Stephen

PEACE,
beetle bailey

by
mort walker

tempo books
GROSSET & DUNLAP
A Filmways Company
Publishers • New York

PEACE, BEETLE BAILEY (#20)

Copyright © 1978, 1979, 1981 by King Features Syndicate, Inc.
All Rights Reserved
ISBN: 0-448-17304-2
An Ace Tempo Original
Tempo Books is registered in the U.S. Patent Office
Published simultaneously in Canada
Printed in the United States of America

Peace, BEETLE BAILEY

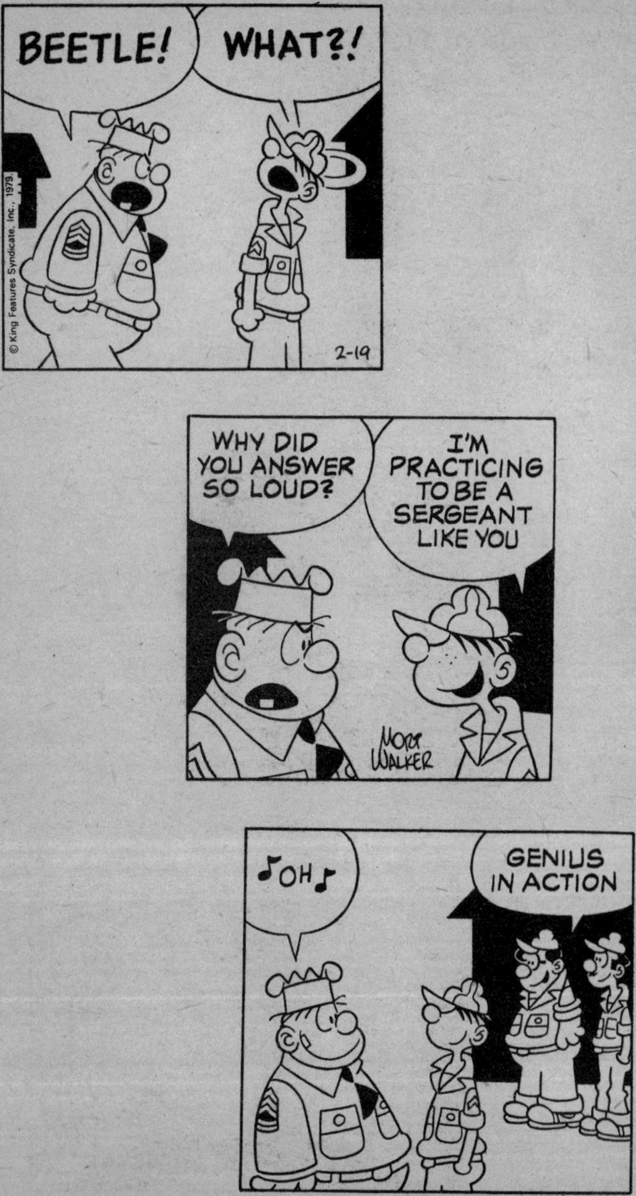

BEETLE!
WHAT?!
© King Features Syndicate, Inc., 1979.
2-19
WHY DID YOU ANSWER SO LOUD?
I'M PRACTICING TO BE A SERGEANT LIKE YOU
MORT WALKER
♪OH♪
GENIUS IN ACTION

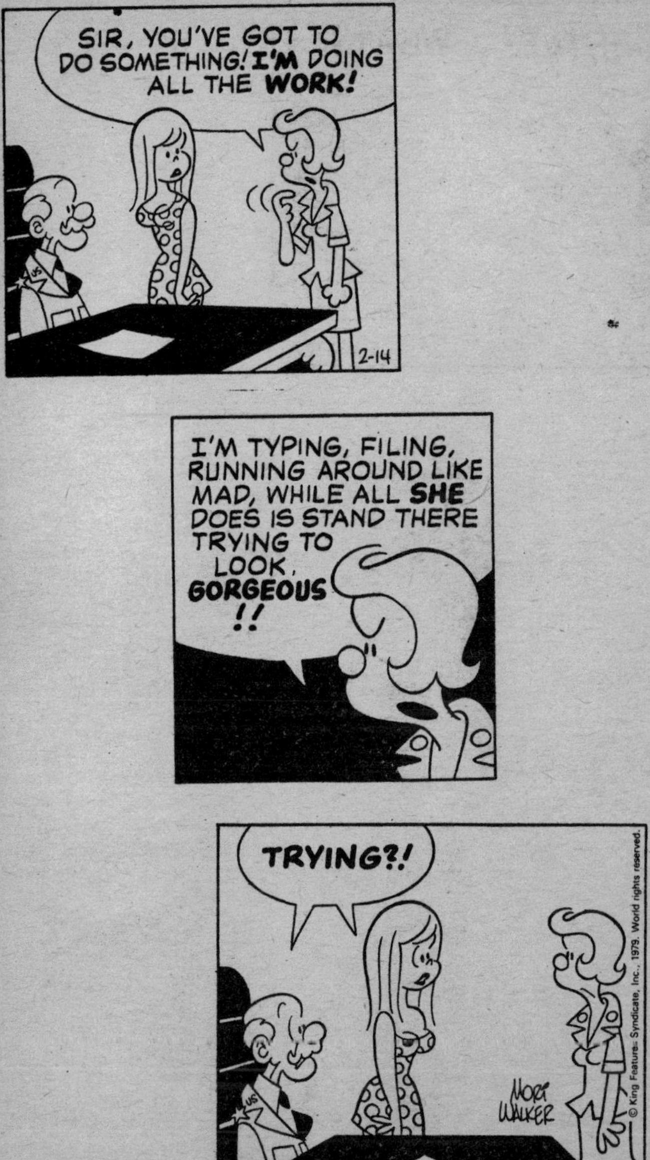
SIR, YOU'VE GOT TO DO SOMETHING! **I'M** DOING ALL THE **WORK!**
2-14
I'M TYPING, FILING, RUNNING AROUND LIKE MAD, WHILE ALL **SHE** DOES IS STAND THERE TRYING TO LOOK **GORGEOUS!!**
TRYING?!
MORT WALKER

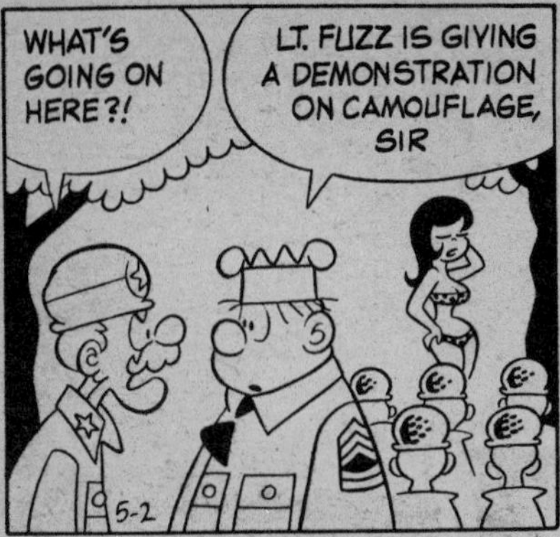
WHAT'S GOING ON HERE?!
LT. FUZZ IS GIVING A DEMONSTRATION ON CAMOUFLAGE, SIR
5-2

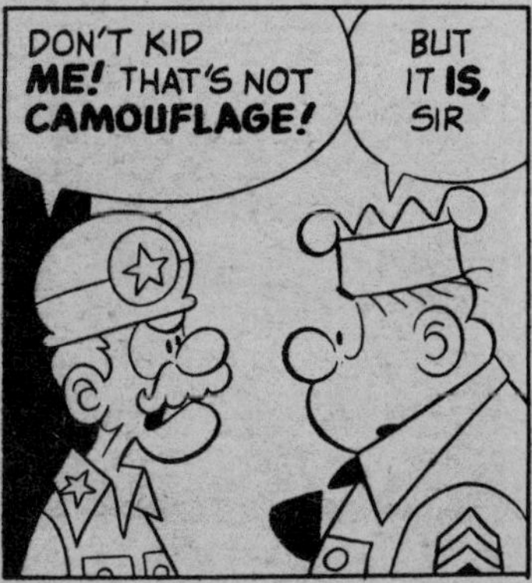
DON'T KID **ME!** THAT'S NOT **CAMOUFLAGE!**
BUT IT **IS,** SIR

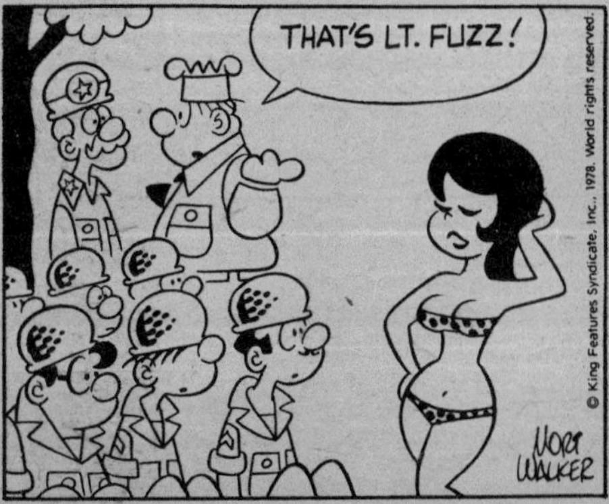
THAT'S LT. FUZZ!
MORT WALKER

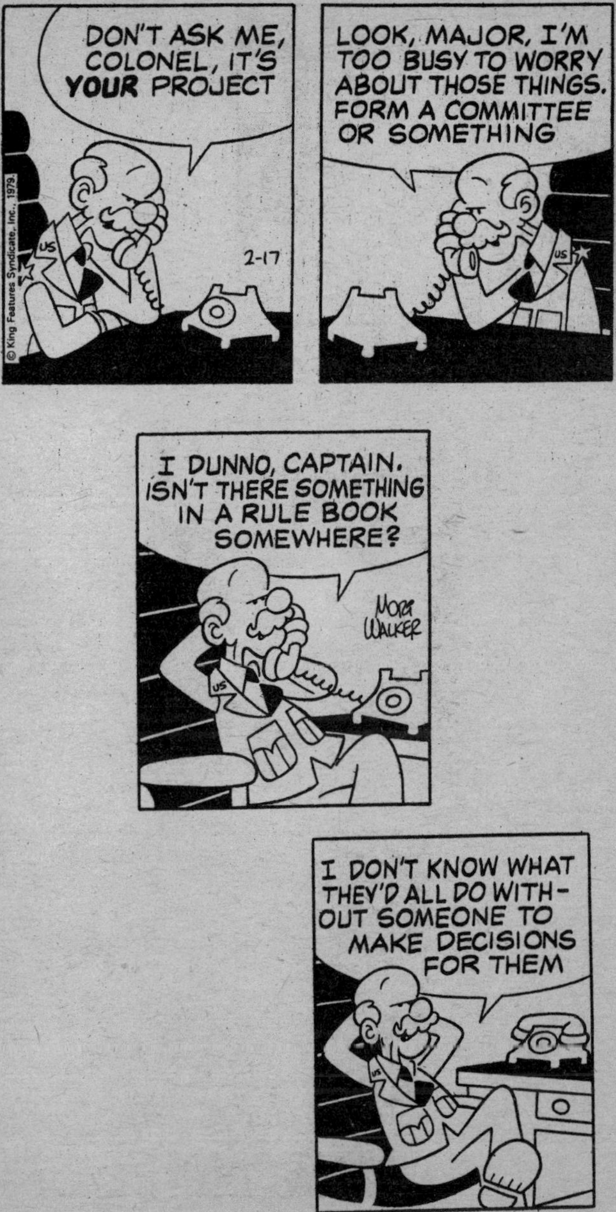
DON'T ASK ME, COLONEL, IT'S **YOUR** PROJECT
© King Features Syndicate, Inc., 1979.
2-17
LOOK, MAJOR, I'M TOO BUSY TO WORRY ABOUT THOSE THINGS. FORM A COMMITTEE OR SOMETHING
I DUNNO, CAPTAIN. ISN'T THERE SOMETHING IN A RULE BOOK SOMEWHERE?
MORT WALKER
I DON'T KNOW WHAT THEY'D ALL DO WITH-OUT SOMEONE TO MAKE DECISIONS FOR THEM

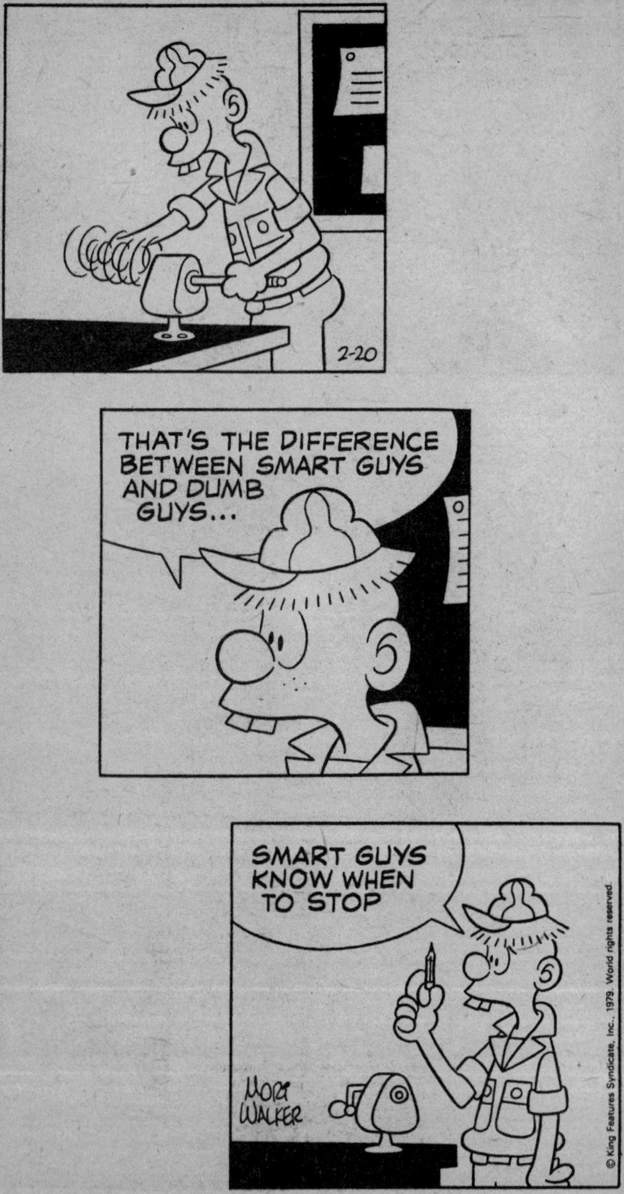
2-20
THAT'S THE DIFFERENCE BETWEEN SMART GUYS AND DUMB GUYS...
SMART GUYS KNOW WHEN TO STOP
MORT WALKER
© King Features Syndicate, Inc., 1979. World rights reserved.

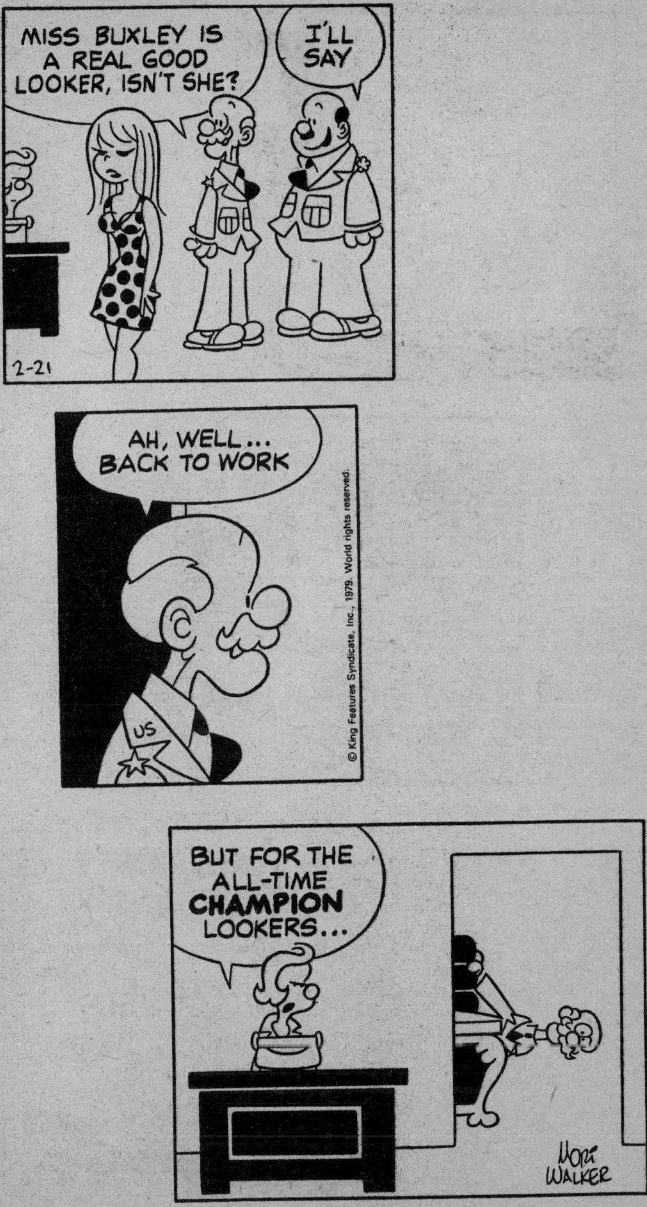
MISS BUXLEY IS A REAL GOOD LOOKER, ISN'T SHE?
I'LL SAY
2-21
AH, WELL... BACK TO WORK
US
© King Features Syndicate, Inc., 1979. World rights reserved.
BUT FOR THE ALL-TIME CHAMPION LOOKERS...
MORT WALKER

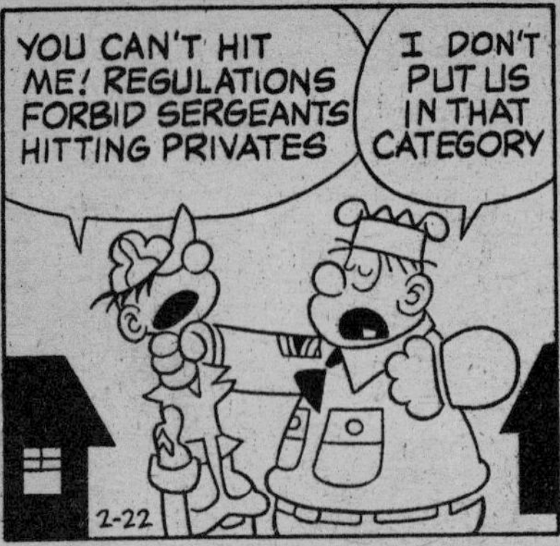
YOU CAN'T HIT ME! REGULATIONS FORBID SERGEANTS HITTING PRIVATES
I DON'T PUT US IN THAT CATEGORY
2-22

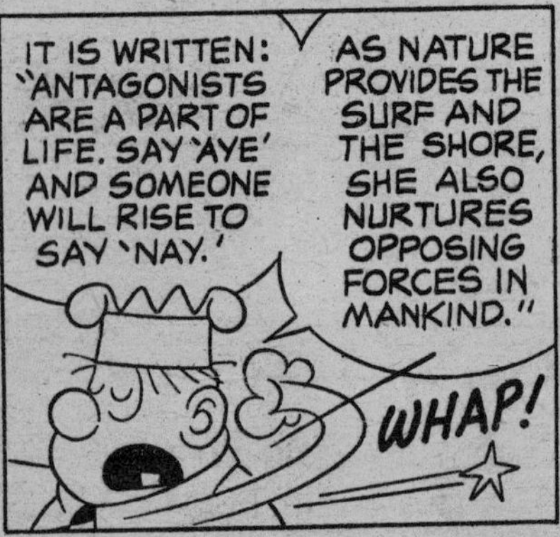
IT IS WRITTEN: "ANTAGONISTS ARE A PART OF LIFE. SAY 'AYE' AND SOMEONE WILL RISE TO SAY 'NAY.'
AS NATURE PROVIDES THE SURF AND THE SHORE, SHE ALSO NURTURES OPPOSING FORCES IN MANKIND."
WHAP!

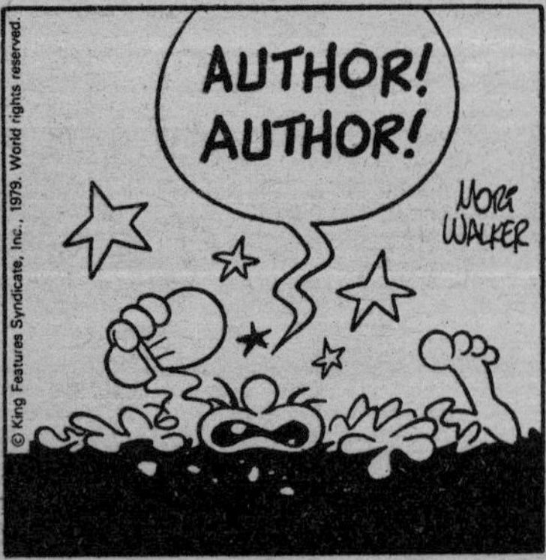
AUTHOR! AUTHOR!
MORT WALKER

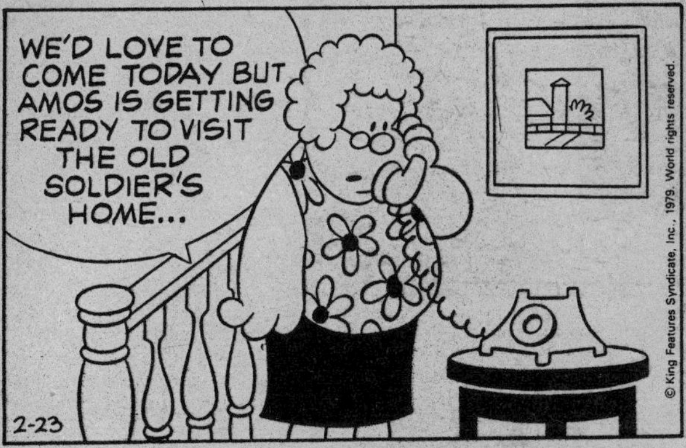
WE'D LOVE TO COME TODAY BUT AMOS IS GETTING READY TO VISIT THE OLD SOLDIER'S HOME...
2-23
© King Features Syndicate, Inc., 1979. World rights reserved.

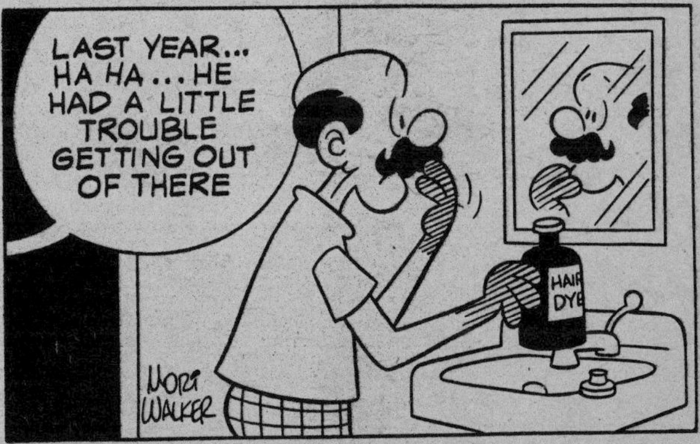
LAST YEAR... HA HA... HE HAD A LITTLE TROUBLE GETTING OUT OF THERE
HAIR DYE
MORT WALKER

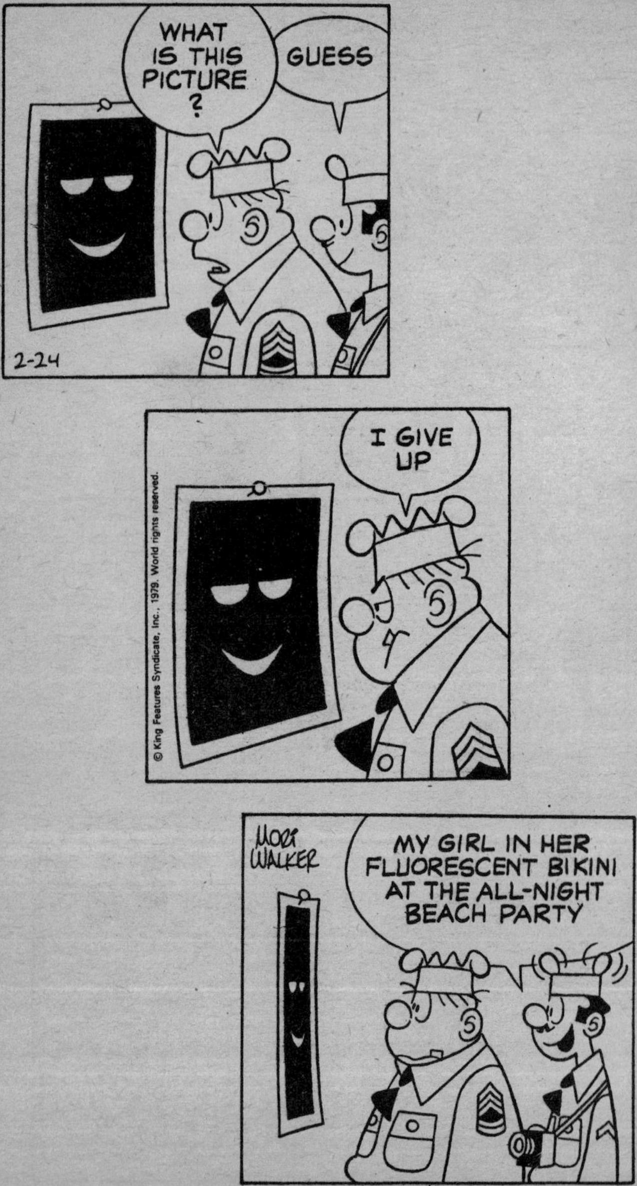
WHAT IS THIS PICTURE ?
GUESS
2-24
I GIVE UP
MORT WALKER
MY GIRL IN HER FLUORESCENT BIKINI AT THE ALL-NIGHT BEACH PARTY

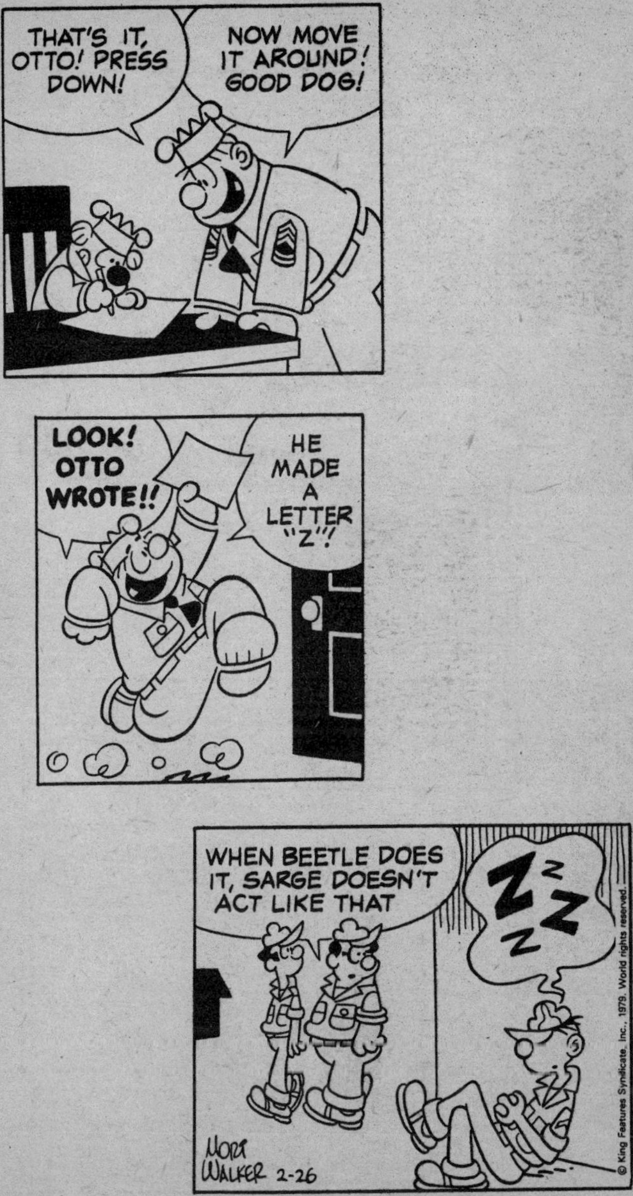
THAT'S IT, OTTO! PRESS DOWN!
NOW MOVE IT AROUND! GOOD DOG!
LOOK! OTTO WROTE!!
HE MADE A LETTER "Z"!
WHEN BEETLE DOES IT, SARGE DOESN'T ACT LIKE THAT
Z Z Z Z
MORT WALKER 2-26
© King Features Syndicate, Inc., 1979. World rights reserved.

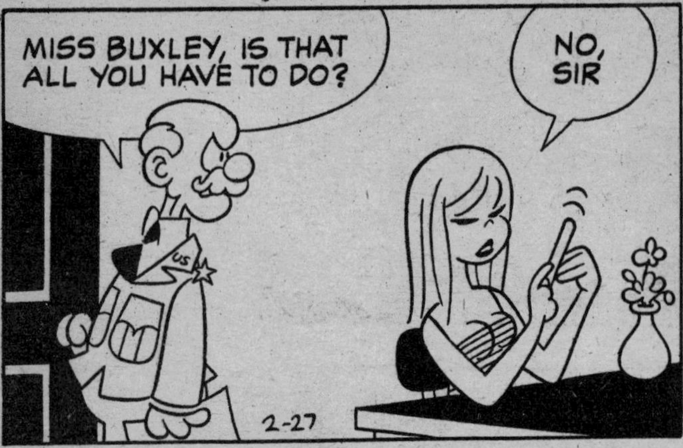
MISS BUXLEY, IS THAT ALL YOU HAVE TO DO?
NO, SIR
US
2-27

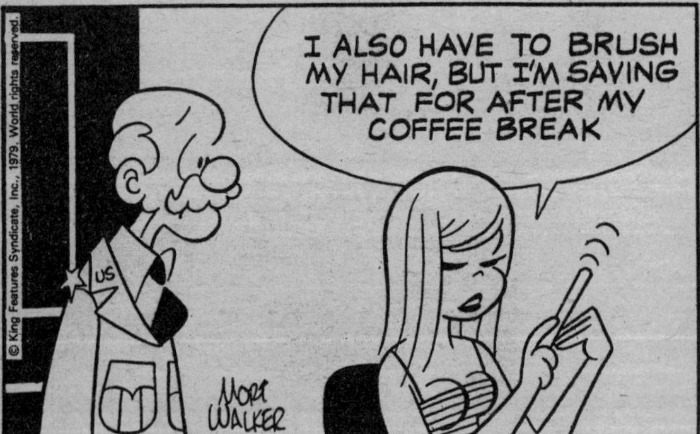
I ALSO HAVE TO BRUSH MY HAIR, BUT I'M SAVING THAT FOR AFTER MY COFFEE BREAK
US
MORT WALKER
© King Features Syndicate, Inc., 1979. World rights reserved.

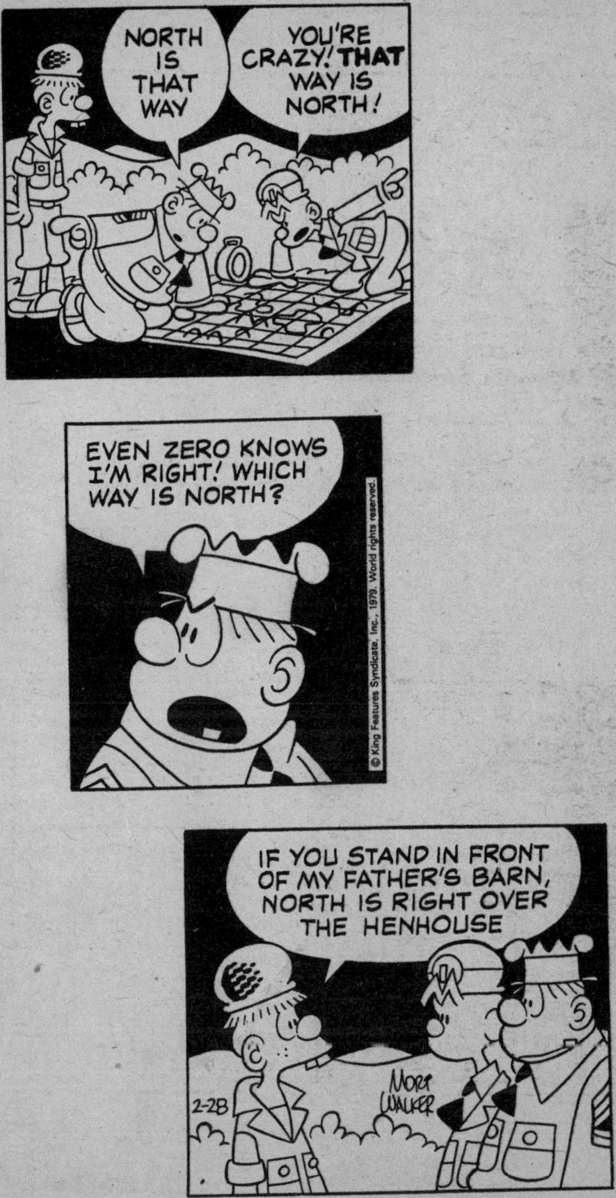
NORTH IS THAT WAY
YOU'RE CRAZY! THAT WAY IS NORTH!
EVEN ZERO KNOWS I'M RIGHT! WHICH WAY IS NORTH?
© King Features Syndicate, Inc., 1979. World rights reserved.
IF YOU STAND IN FRONT OF MY FATHER'S BARN, NORTH IS RIGHT OVER THE HENHOUSE
2-28
MORT WALKER

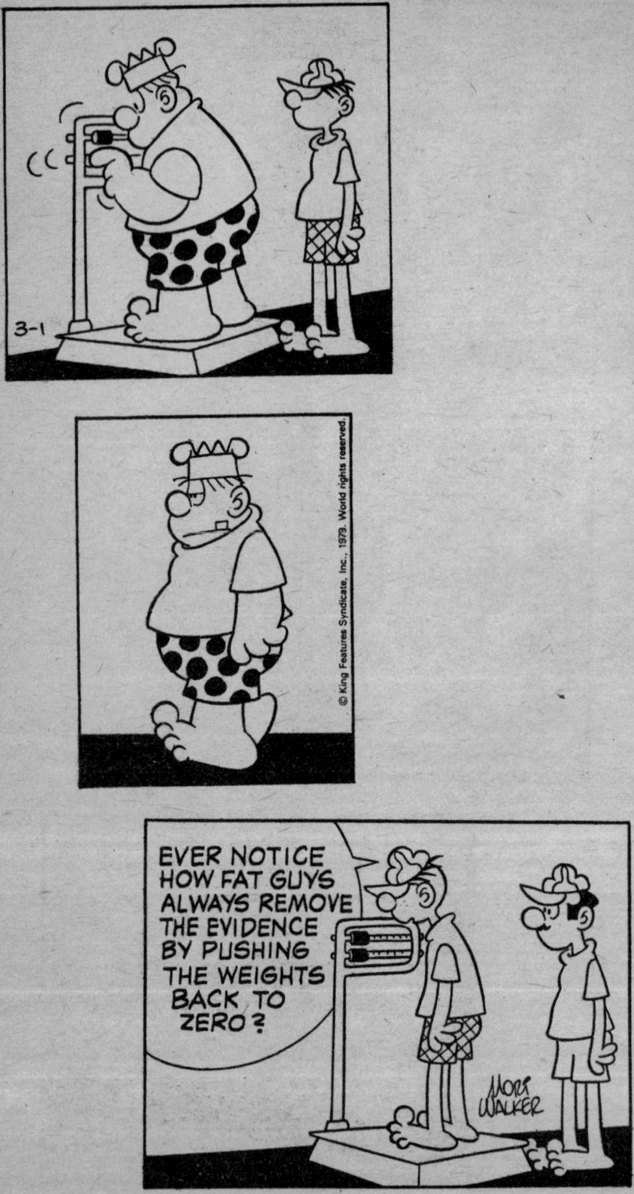
3-1
EVER NOTICE HOW FAT GUYS ALWAYS REMOVE THE EVIDENCE BY PUSHING THE WEIGHTS BACK TO ZERO?
MORT WALKER

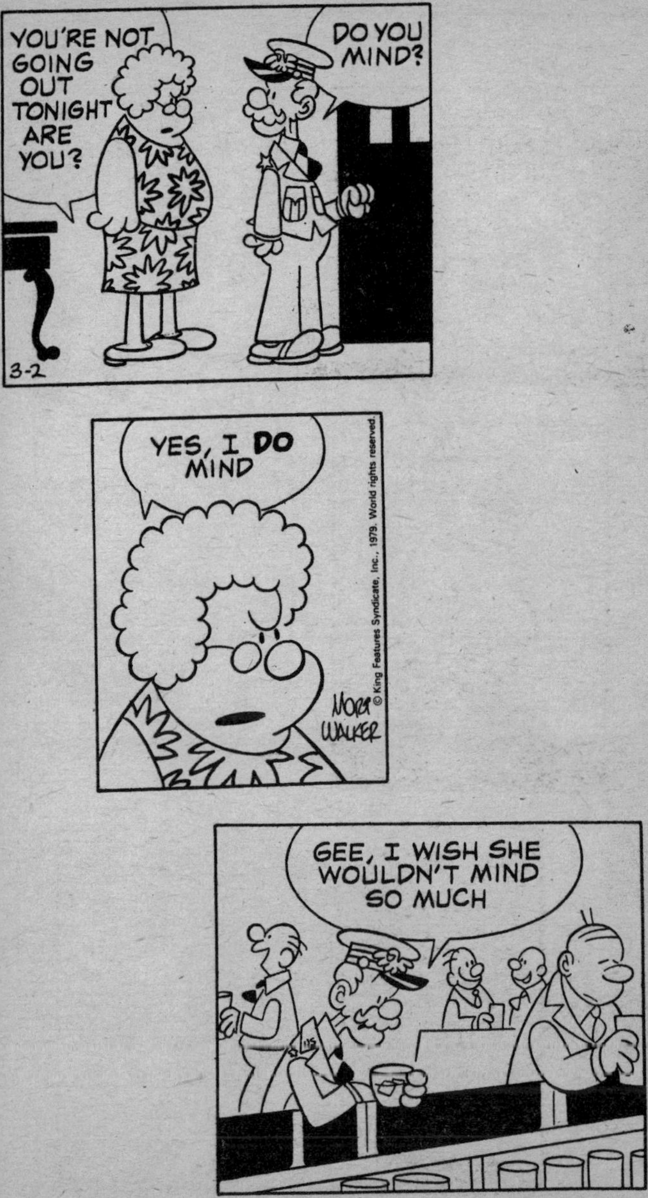
YOU'RE NOT GOING OUT TONIGHT ARE YOU?
DO YOU MIND?
3-2
YES, I DO MIND
© King Features Syndicate, Inc., 1979. World rights reserved.
MORT WALKER
GEE, I WISH SHE WOULDN'T MIND SO MUCH

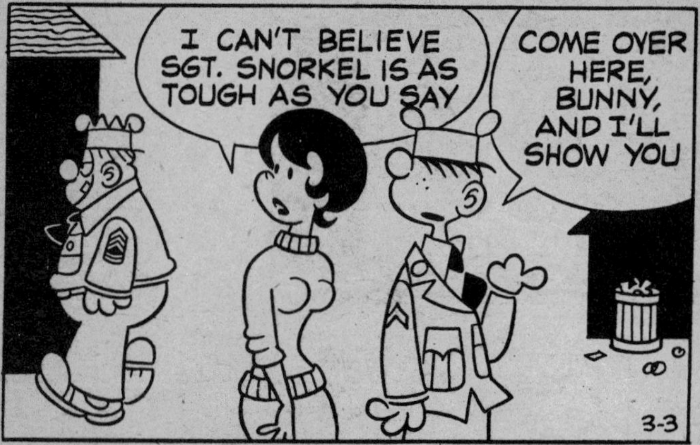
I CAN'T BELIEVE SGT. SNORKEL IS AS TOUGH AS YOU SAY
COME OVER HERE, BUNNY, AND I'LL SHOW YOU
3-3

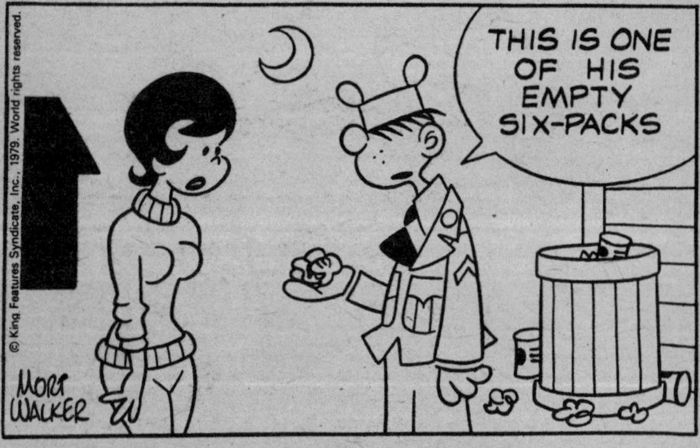
THIS IS ONE OF HIS EMPTY SIX-PACKS
© King Features Syndicate, Inc., 1979. World rights reserved.
MORT WALKER

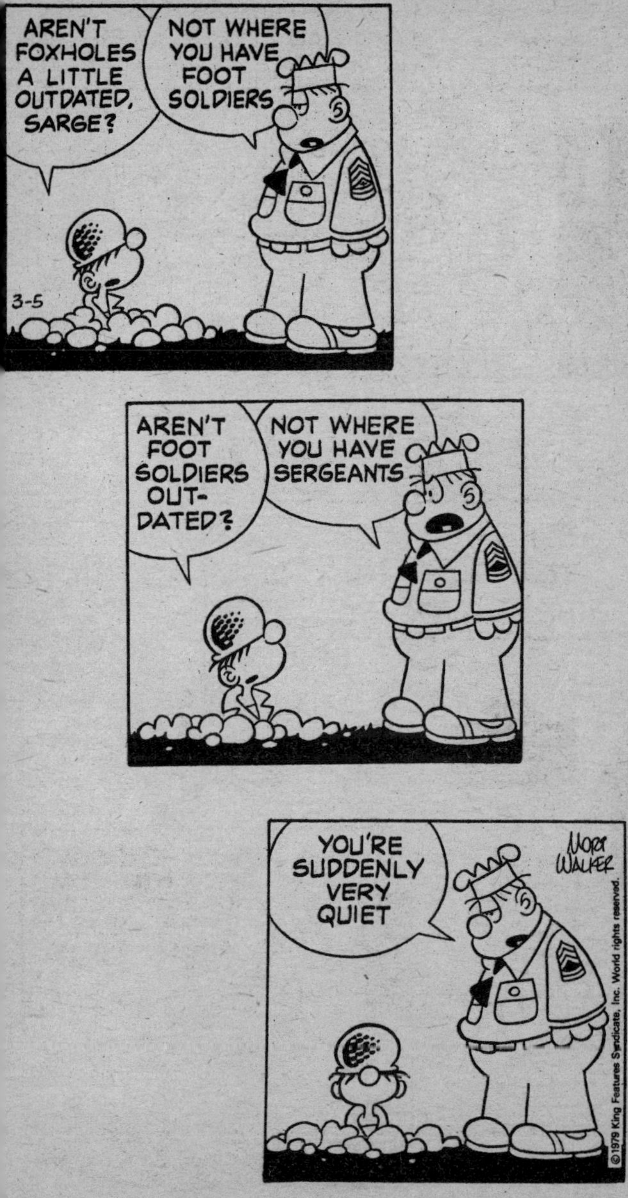
AREN'T FOXHOLES A LITTLE OUTDATED, SARGE?
NOT WHERE YOU HAVE FOOT SOLDIERS
3-5
AREN'T FOOT SOLDIERS OUT-DATED?
NOT WHERE YOU HAVE SERGEANTS
YOU'RE SUDDENLY VERY QUIET
MORT WALKER
©1979 King Features Syndicate, Inc. World rights reserved.

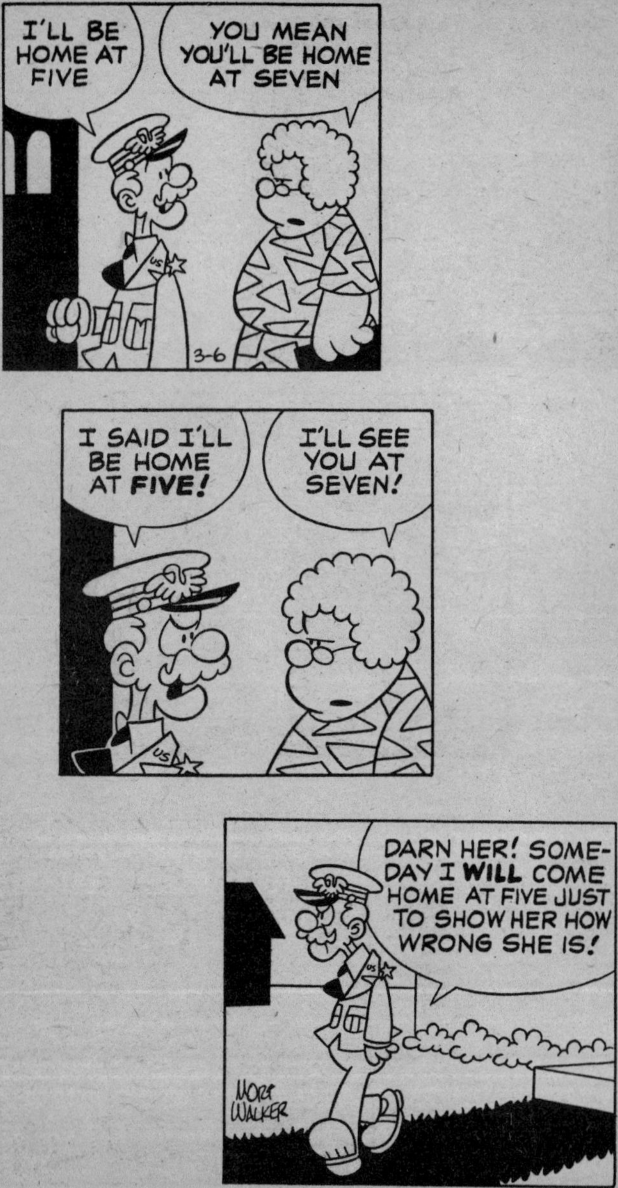
I'LL BE HOME AT FIVE
YOU MEAN YOU'LL BE HOME AT SEVEN
3-6
I SAID I'LL BE HOME AT FIVE!
I'LL SEE YOU AT SEVEN!
DARN HER! SOMEDAY I WILL COME HOME AT FIVE JUST TO SHOW HER HOW WRONG SHE IS!
MORT WALKER

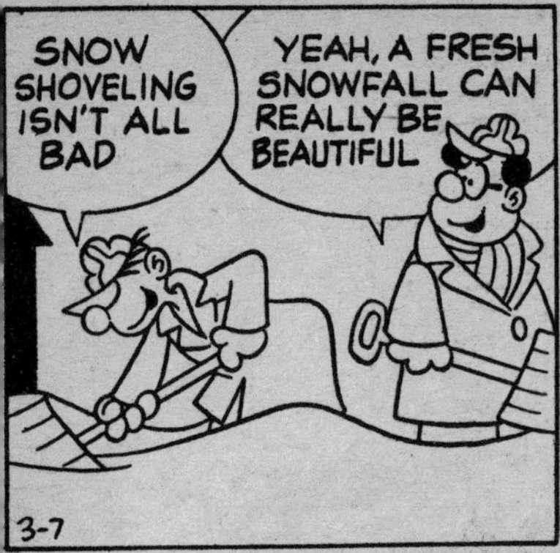
SNOW SHOVELING ISN'T ALL BAD
YEAH, A FRESH SNOWFALL CAN REALLY BE BEAUTIFUL
3-7

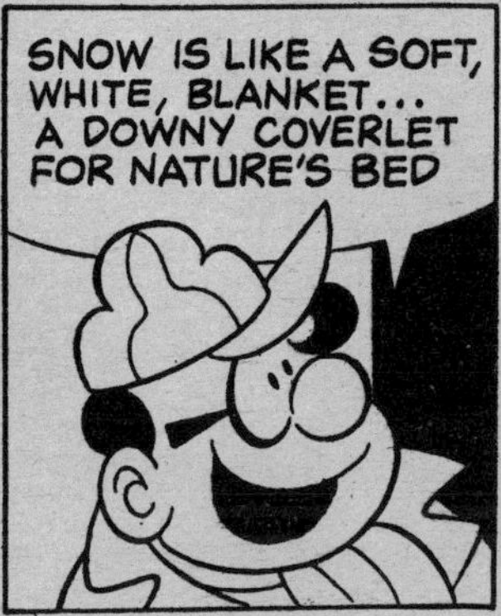
SNOW IS LIKE A SOFT, WHITE, BLANKET... A DOWNY COVERLET FOR NATURE'S BED

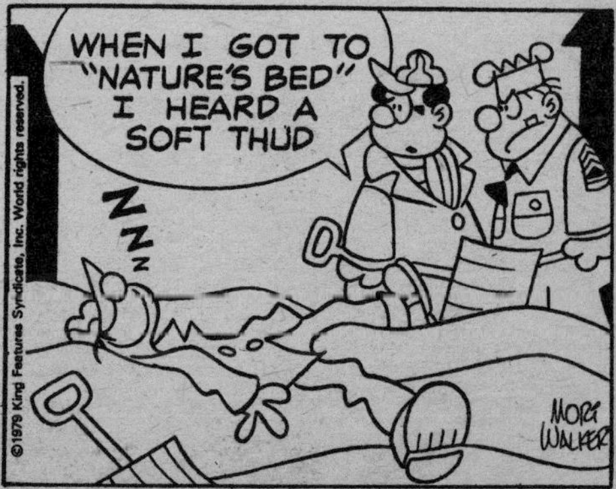
WHEN I GOT TO "NATURE'S BED" I HEARD A SOFT THUD
ZZZ
MORT WALKER
©1979 King Features Syndicate, Inc. World rights reserved.

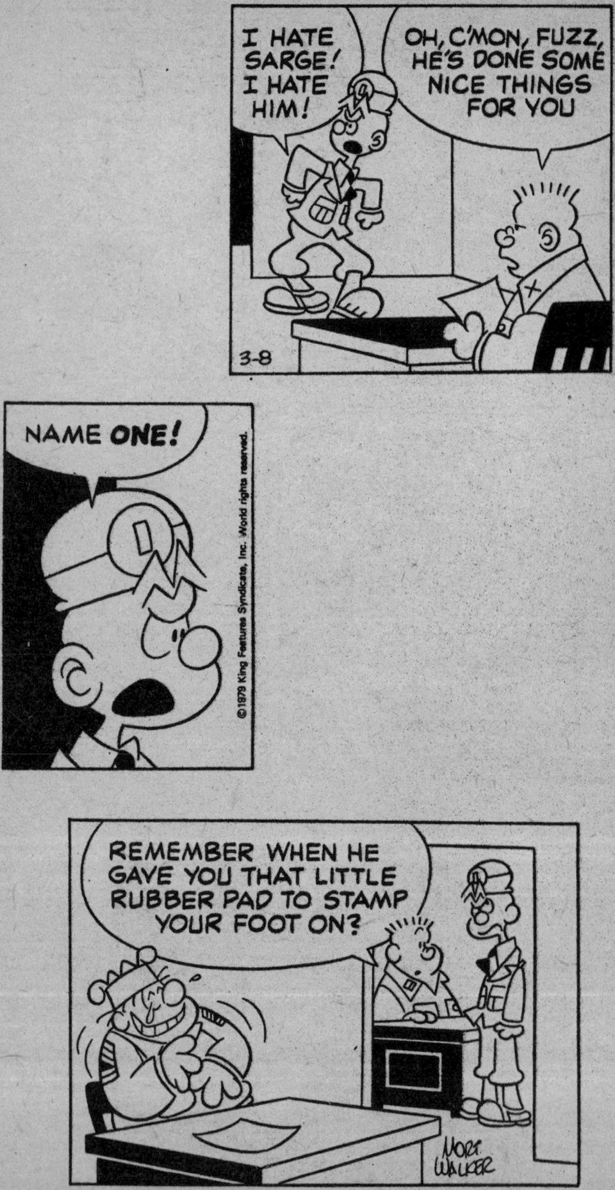
I HATE SARGE! I HATE HIM!
OH, C'MON, FUZZ, HE'S DONE SOME NICE THINGS FOR YOU
3-8
NAME ONE!
©1979 King Features Syndicate, Inc. World rights reserved.
REMEMBER WHEN HE GAVE YOU THAT LITTLE RUBBER PAD TO STAMP YOUR FOOT ON?
MORT WALKER

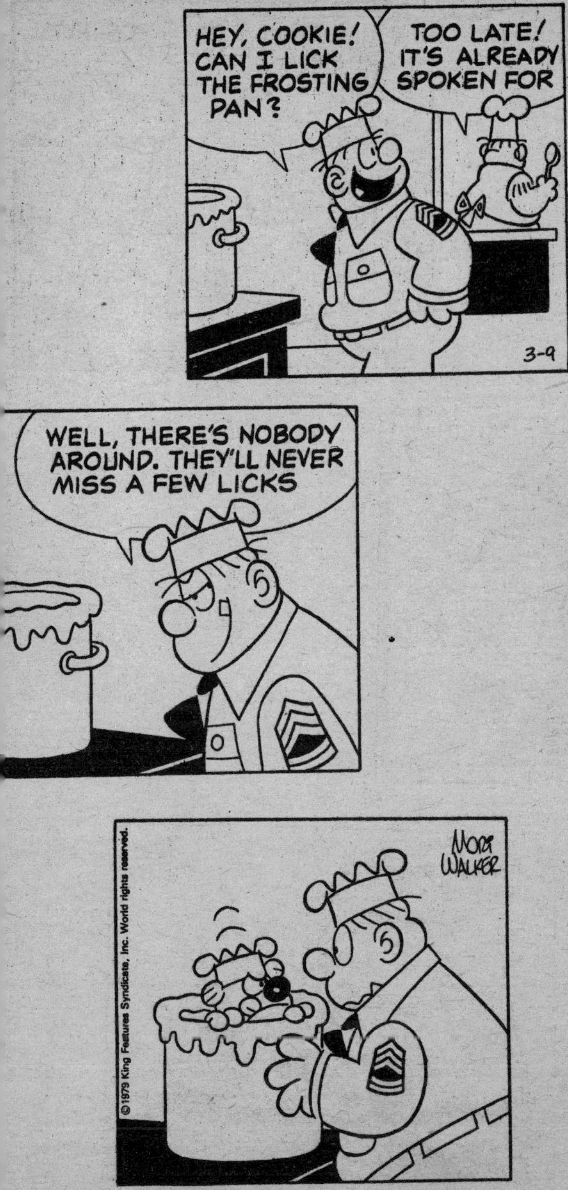
HEY, COOKIE! CAN I LICK THE FROSTING PAN?
TOO LATE! IT'S ALREADY SPOKEN FOR
3-9
WELL, THERE'S NOBODY AROUND. THEY'LL NEVER MISS A FEW LICKS
MORT WALKER
©1979 King Features Syndicate, Inc. World rights reserved.

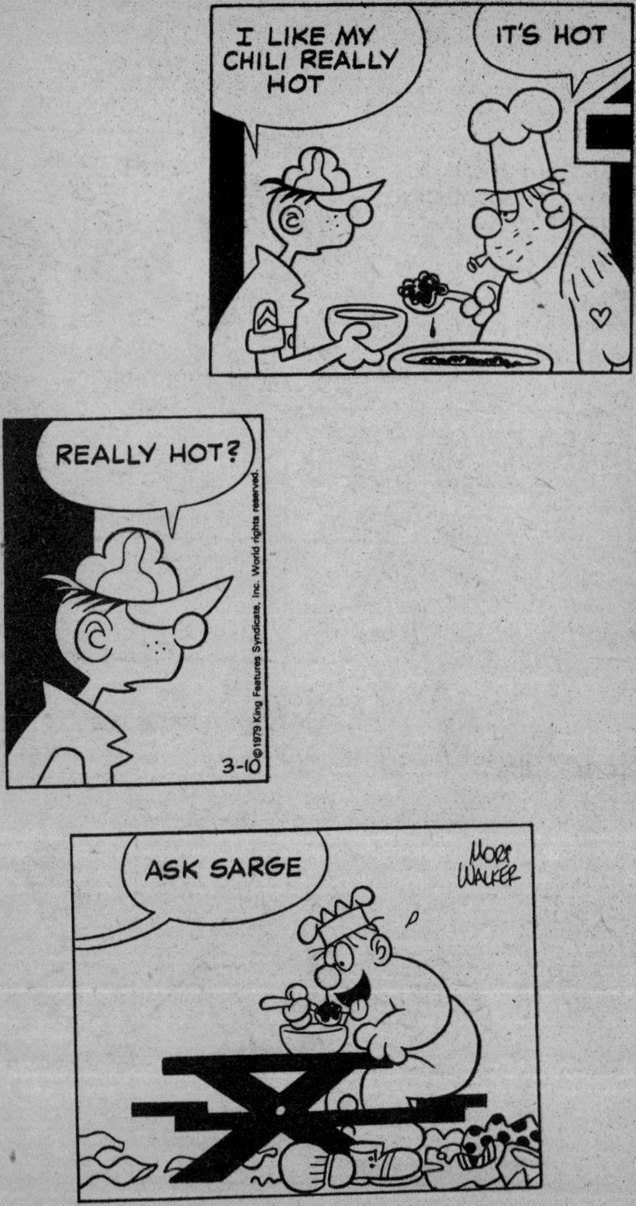
I LIKE MY CHILI REALLY HOT
IT'S HOT
REALLY HOT?
©1979 King Features Syndicate, Inc. World rights reserved.
3-10
ASK SARGE
MORT WALKER

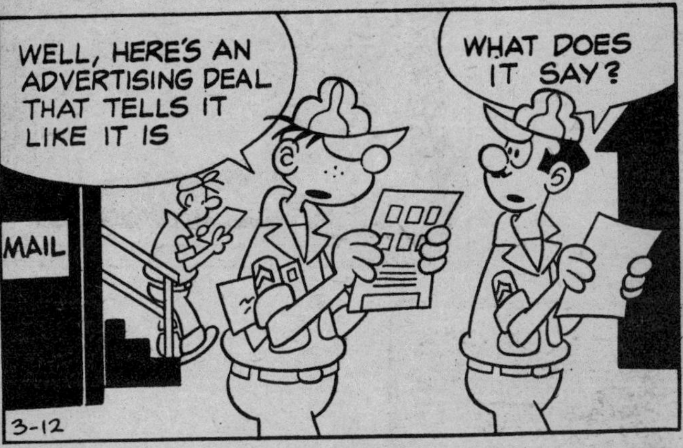
WELL, HERE'S AN ADVERTISING DEAL THAT TELLS IT LIKE IT IS
WHAT DOES IT SAY?
MAIL
3-12

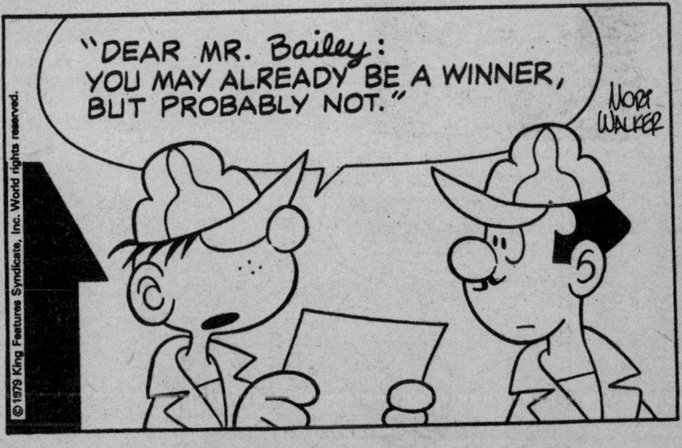
"DEAR MR. Bailey:
YOU MAY ALREADY BE A WINNER, BUT PROBABLY NOT."
NORT WALKER
© 1979 King Features Syndicate, Inc. World rights reserved.

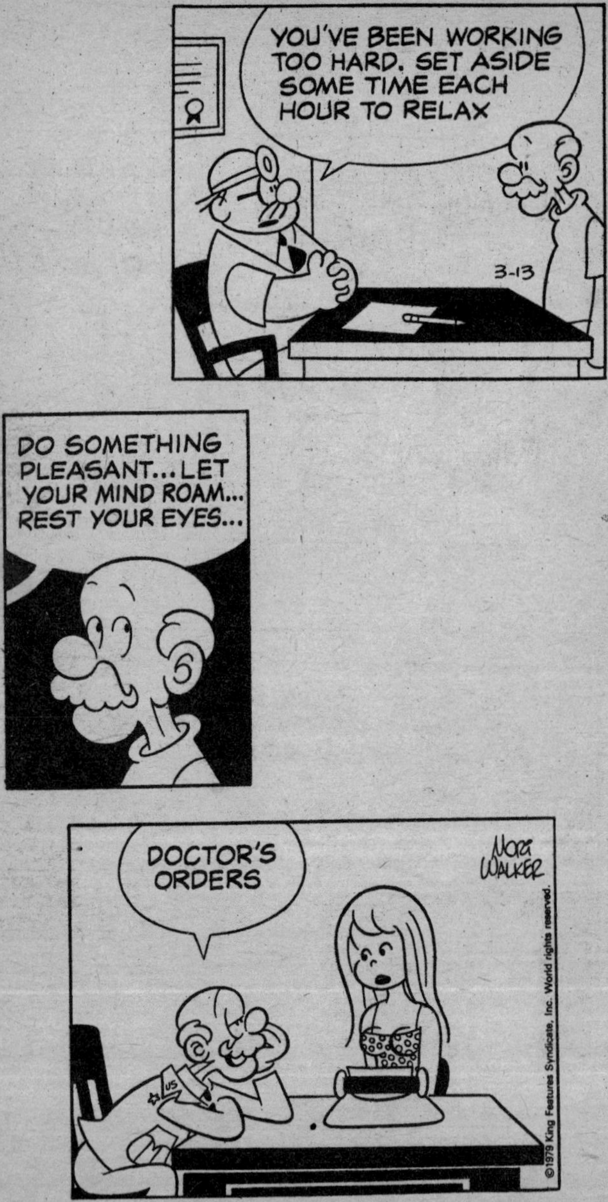
YOU'VE BEEN WORKING TOO HARD. SET ASIDE SOME TIME EACH HOUR TO RELAX
3-13
DO SOMETHING PLEASANT...LET YOUR MIND ROAM... REST YOUR EYES...
DOCTOR'S ORDERS
US
©1979 King Features Syndicate, Inc. World rights reserved.

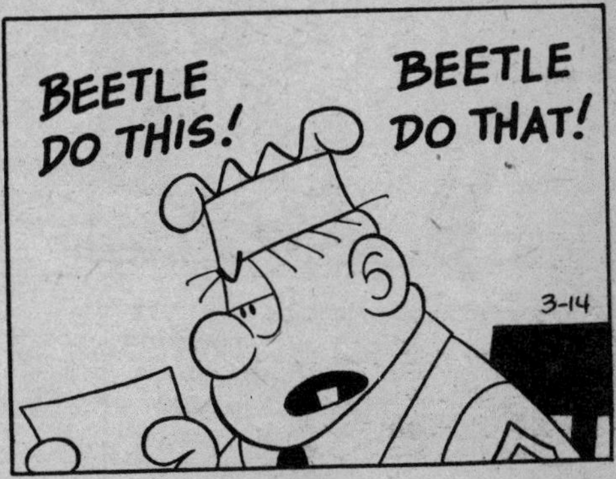
BEETLE DO THIS!
BEETLE DO THAT!
3-14

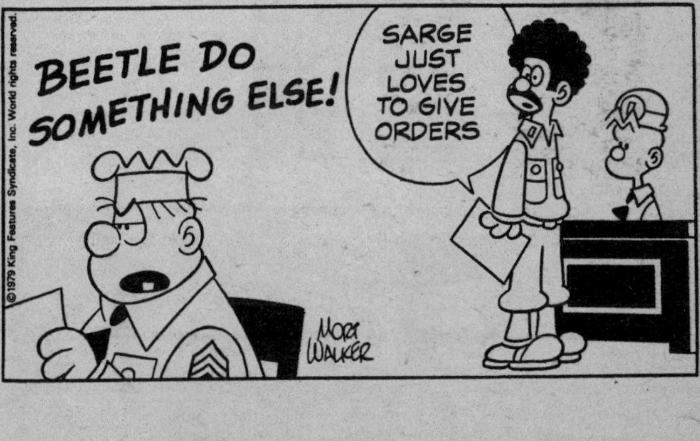
BEETLE DO SOMETHING ELSE!
SARGE JUST LOVES TO GIVE ORDERS
MORT WALKER
©1979 King Features Syndicate, Inc. World rights reserved.

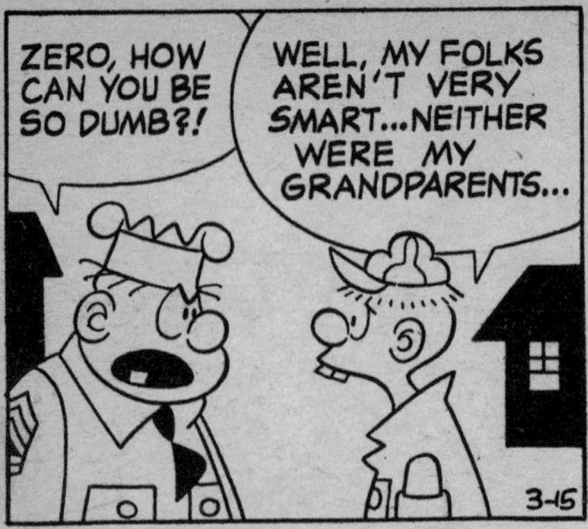
ZERO, HOW CAN YOU BE SO DUMB?!
WELL, MY FOLKS AREN'T VERY SMART...NEITHER WERE MY GRANDPARENTS...
3-15

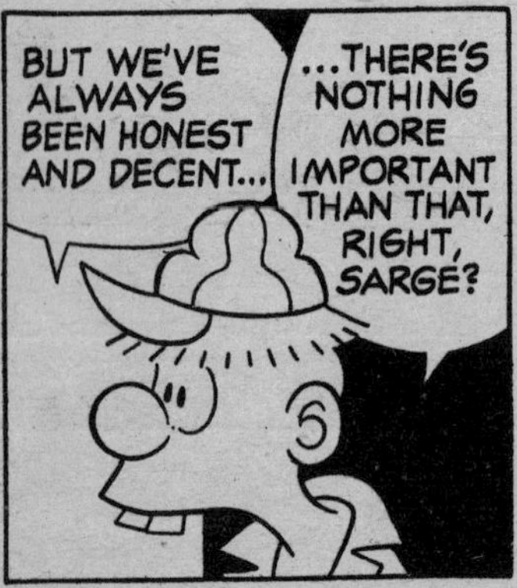
BUT WE'VE ALWAYS BEEN HONEST AND DECENT...
...THERE'S NOTHING MORE IMPORTANT THAN THAT, RIGHT, SARGE?

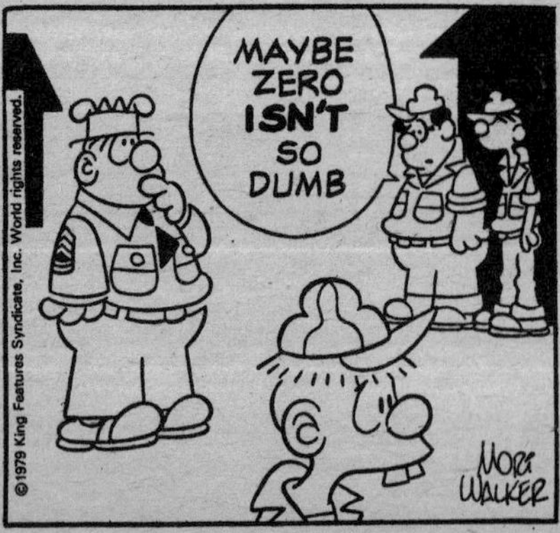
MAYBE ZERO **ISN'T** SO DUMB
©1979 King Features Syndicate, Inc. World rights reserved.
MORT WALKER

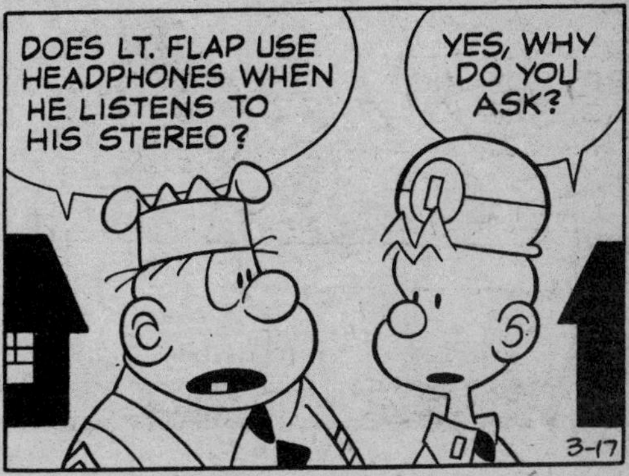
DOES LT. FLAP USE HEADPHONES WHEN HE LISTENS TO HIS STEREO?
YES, WHY DO YOU ASK?
3-17

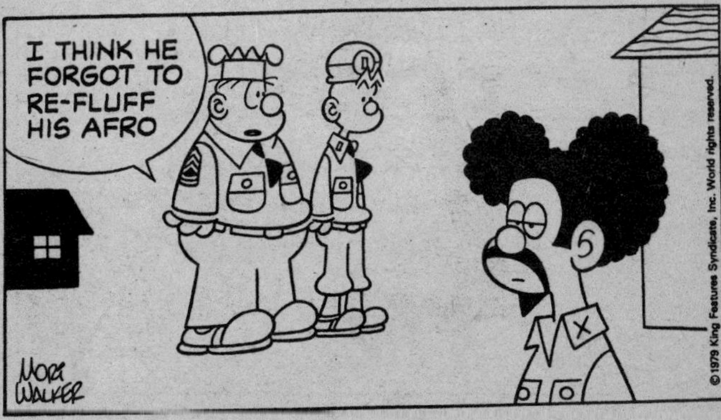
I THINK HE FORGOT TO RE-FLUFF HIS AFRO
MORT WALKER
© 1979 King Features Syndicate, Inc. World rights reserved.

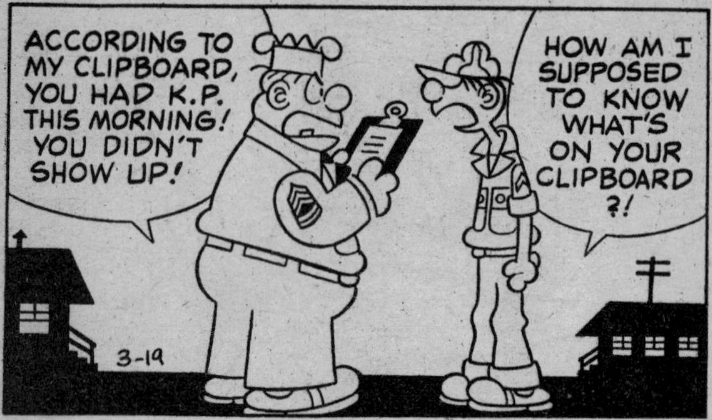
ACCORDING TO MY CLIPBOARD, YOU HAD K.P. THIS MORNING! YOU DIDN'T SHOW UP!
HOW AM I SUPPOSED TO KNOW WHAT'S ON YOUR CLIPBOARD ?!
3-19

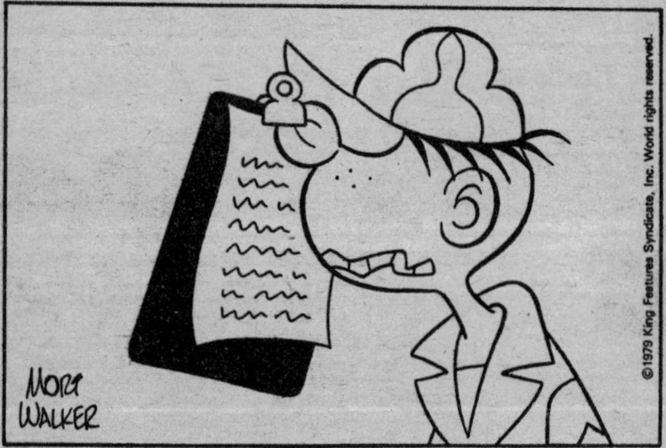
MORT WALKER

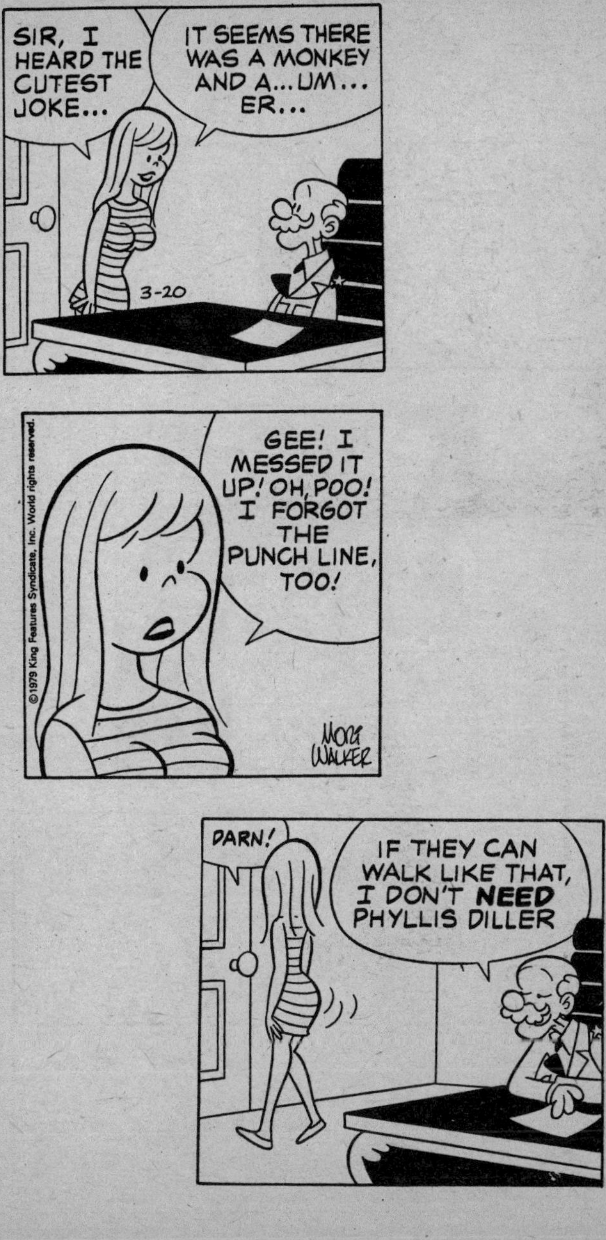
SIR, I HEARD THE CUTEST JOKE...
IT SEEMS THERE WAS A MONKEY AND A...UM... ER...
3-20
GEE! I MESSED IT UP! OH, POO! I FORGOT THE PUNCH LINE, TOO!
©1979 King Features Syndicate, Inc. World rights reserved.
MORT WALKER
DARN!
IF THEY CAN WALK LIKE THAT, I DON'T **NEED** PHYLLIS DILLER

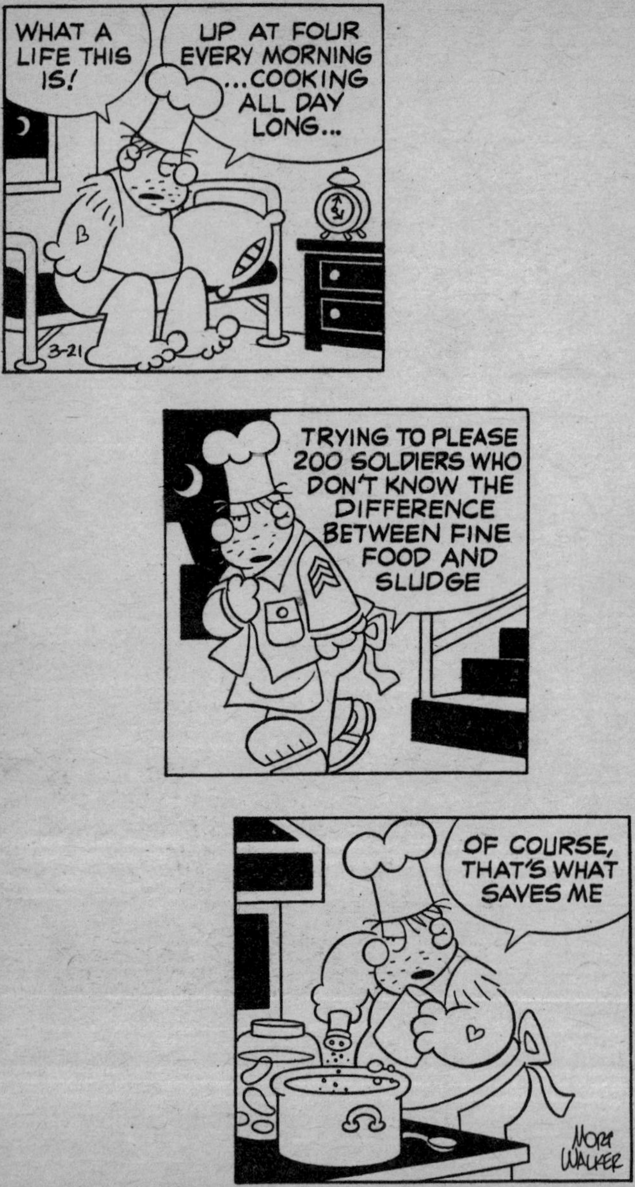
WHAT A LIFE THIS IS!
UP AT FOUR EVERY MORNING ...COOKING ALL DAY LONG...
3-21
TRYING TO PLEASE 200 SOLDIERS WHO DON'T KNOW THE DIFFERENCE BETWEEN FINE FOOD AND SLUDGE
OF COURSE, THAT'S WHAT SAVES ME
MORT WALKER

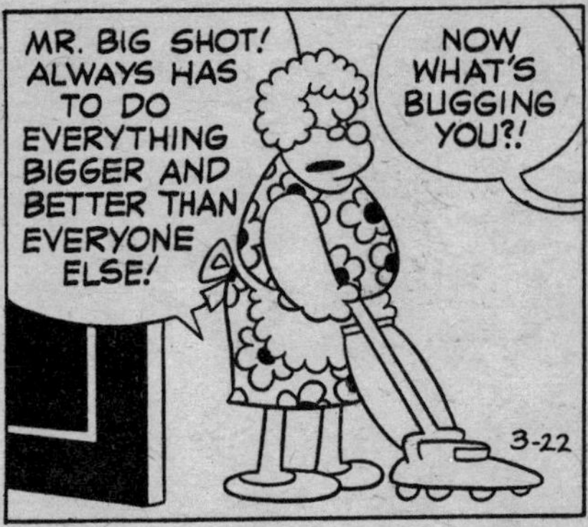
MR. BIG SHOT! ALWAYS HAS TO DO EVERYTHING BIGGER AND BETTER THAN EVERYONE ELSE!
NOW WHAT'S BUGGING YOU?!
3-22

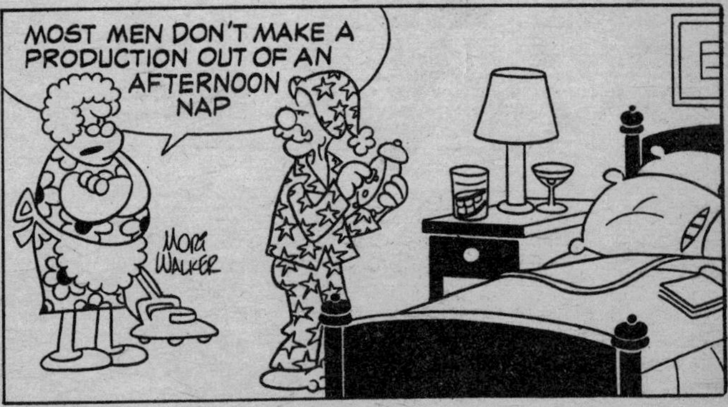
MOST MEN DON'T MAKE A PRODUCTION OUT OF AN AFTERNOON NAP
MORT WALKER

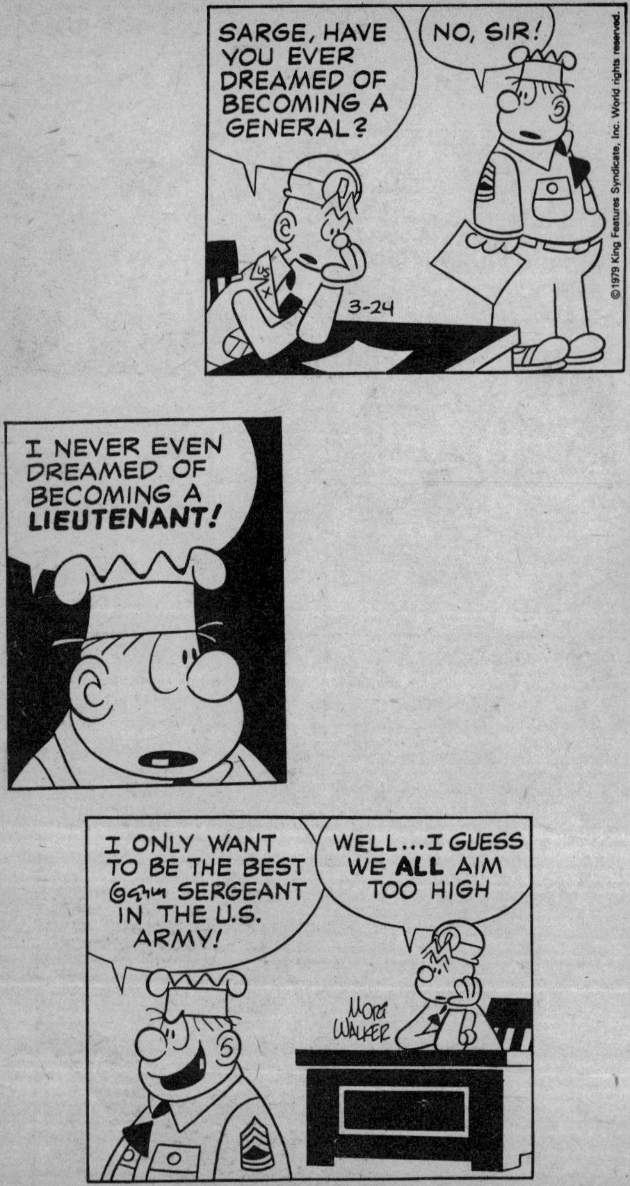
SARGE, HAVE YOU EVER DREAMED OF BECOMING A GENERAL?
NO, SIR!
3-24
©1979 King Features Syndicate, Inc. World rights reserved.
I NEVER EVEN DREAMED OF BECOMING A **LIEUTENANT**!
I ONLY WANT TO BE THE BEST SERGEANT IN THE U.S. ARMY!
WELL...I GUESS WE **ALL** AIM TOO HIGH
MORT WALKER

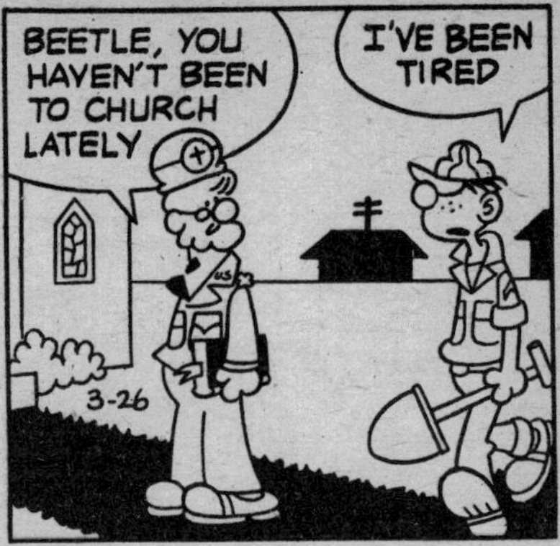
BEETLE, YOU HAVEN'T BEEN TO CHURCH LATELY
I'VE BEEN TIRED
3-26

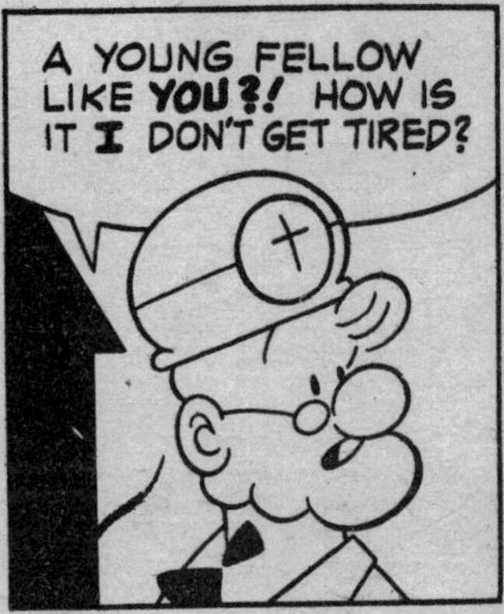
A YOUNG FELLOW LIKE **YOU?!** HOW IS IT **I** DON'T GET TIRED?

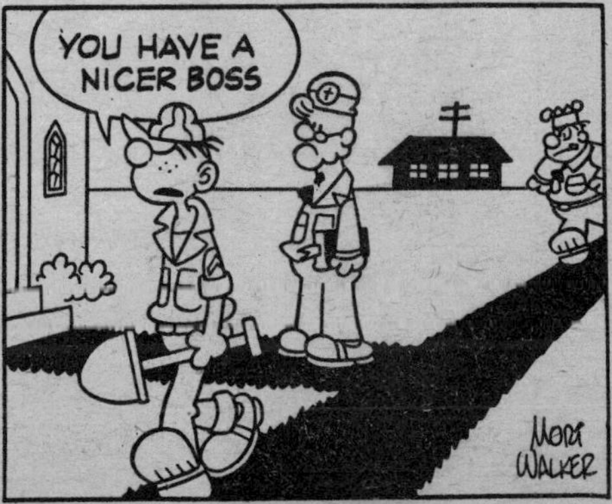
YOU HAVE A NICER BOSS
MORT WALKER

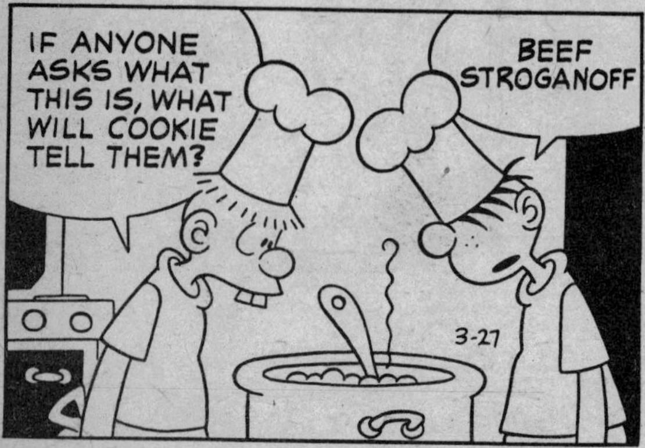
IF ANYONE ASKS WHAT THIS IS, WHAT WILL COOKIE TELL THEM?
BEEF STROGANOFF
3-27

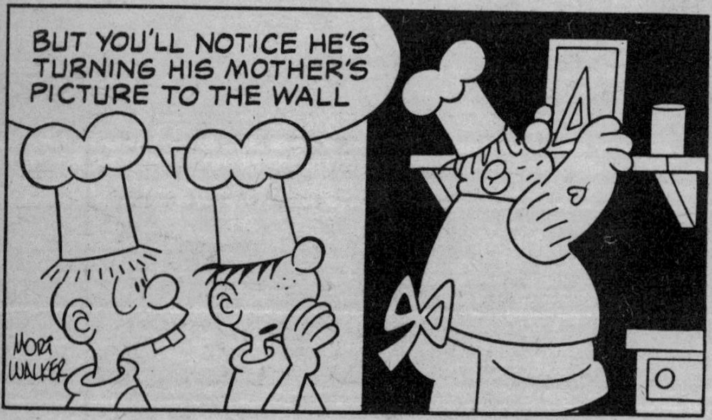
BUT YOU'LL NOTICE HE'S TURNING HIS MOTHER'S PICTURE TO THE WALL
MORT WALKER

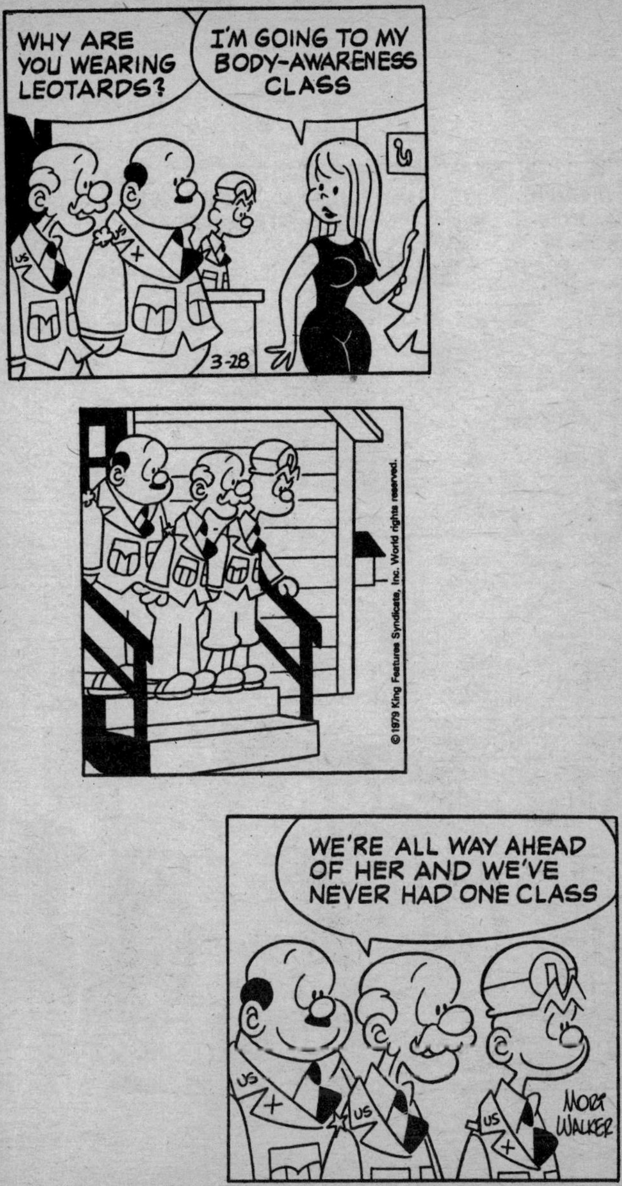
WHY ARE YOU WEARING LEOTARDS?
I'M GOING TO MY BODY-AWARENESS CLASS
3-28
©1979 King Features Syndicate, Inc. World rights reserved.
WE'RE ALL WAY AHEAD OF HER AND WE'VE NEVER HAD ONE CLASS
MORT WALKER

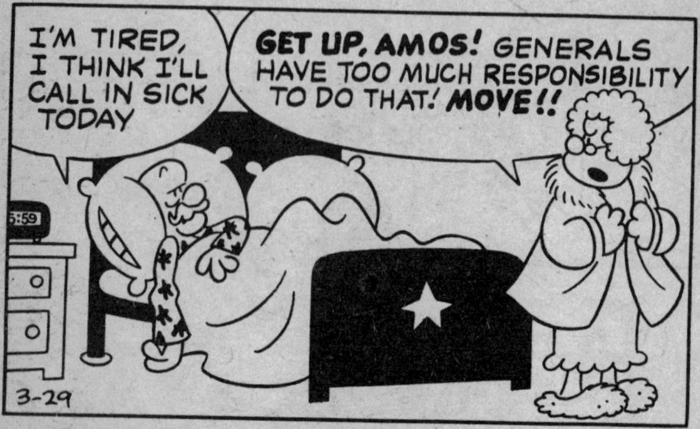
I'M TIRED, I THINK I'LL CALL IN SICK TODAY
GET UP, AMOS! GENERALS HAVE TOO MUCH RESPONSIBILITY TO DO THAT! MOVE!!
5:59
3-29

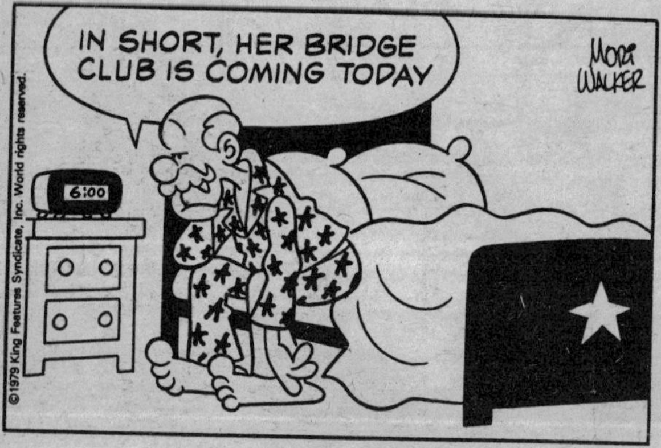
IN SHORT, HER BRIDGE CLUB IS COMING TODAY
6:00
MORT WALKER
©1979 King Features Syndicate, Inc. World rights reserved.

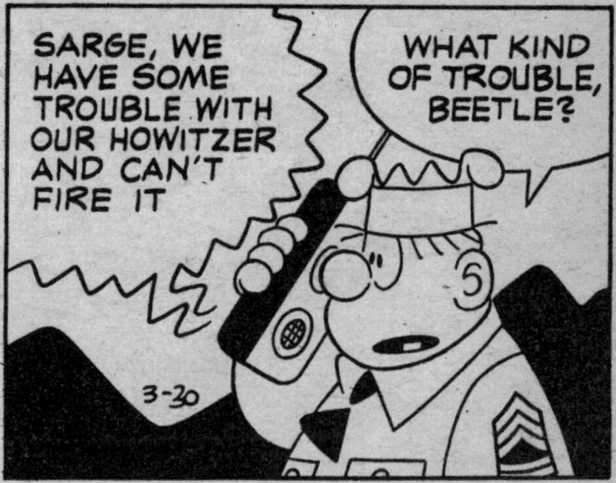
SARGE, WE HAVE SOME TROUBLE WITH OUR HOWITZER AND CAN'T FIRE IT
WHAT KIND OF TROUBLE, BEETLE?
3-30

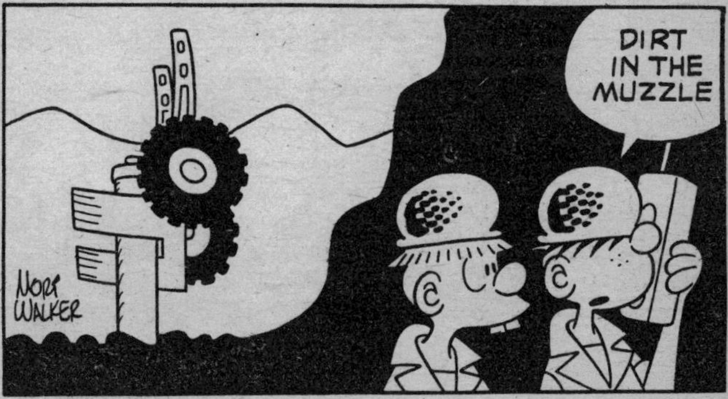
DIRT IN THE MUZZLE
NORT WALKER

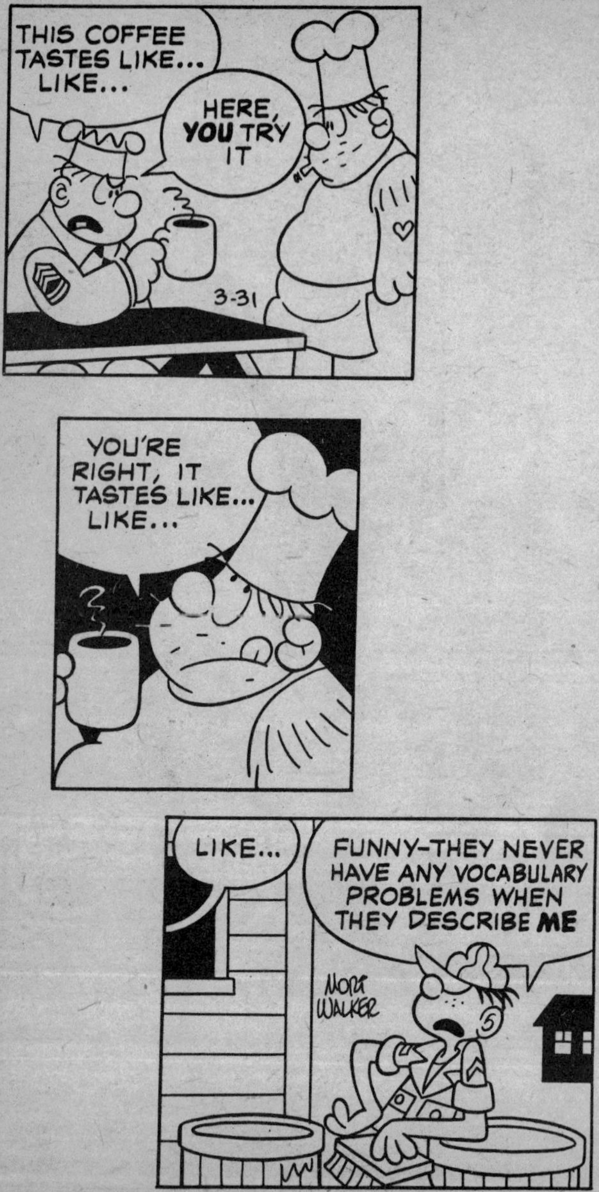
THIS COFFEE TASTES LIKE... LIKE...
HERE, YOU TRY IT
3-31
YOU'RE RIGHT, IT TASTES LIKE... LIKE...
LIKE...
FUNNY—THEY NEVER HAVE ANY VOCABULARY PROBLEMS WHEN THEY DESCRIBE ME
MORT WALKER

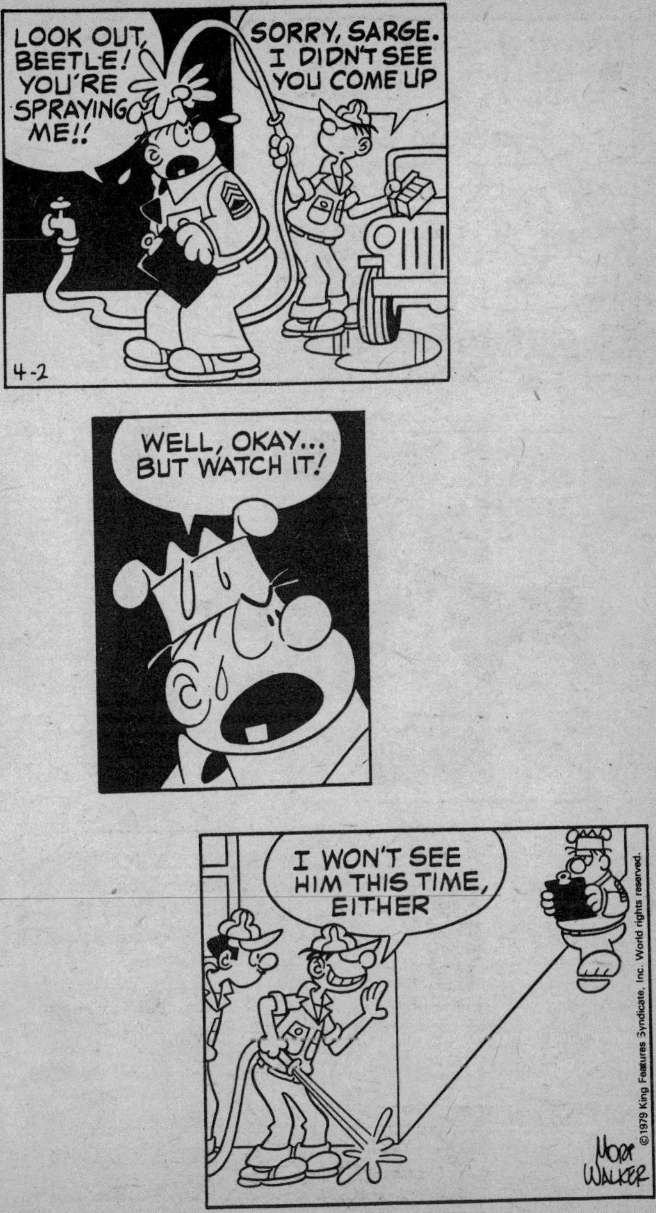
LOOK OUT, BEETLE! YOU'RE SPRAYING ME!!
SORRY, SARGE. I DIDN'T SEE YOU COME UP
4-2
WELL, OKAY... BUT WATCH IT!
I WON'T SEE HIM THIS TIME, EITHER
MORT WALKER
©1979 King Features Syndicate, Inc. World rights reserved.

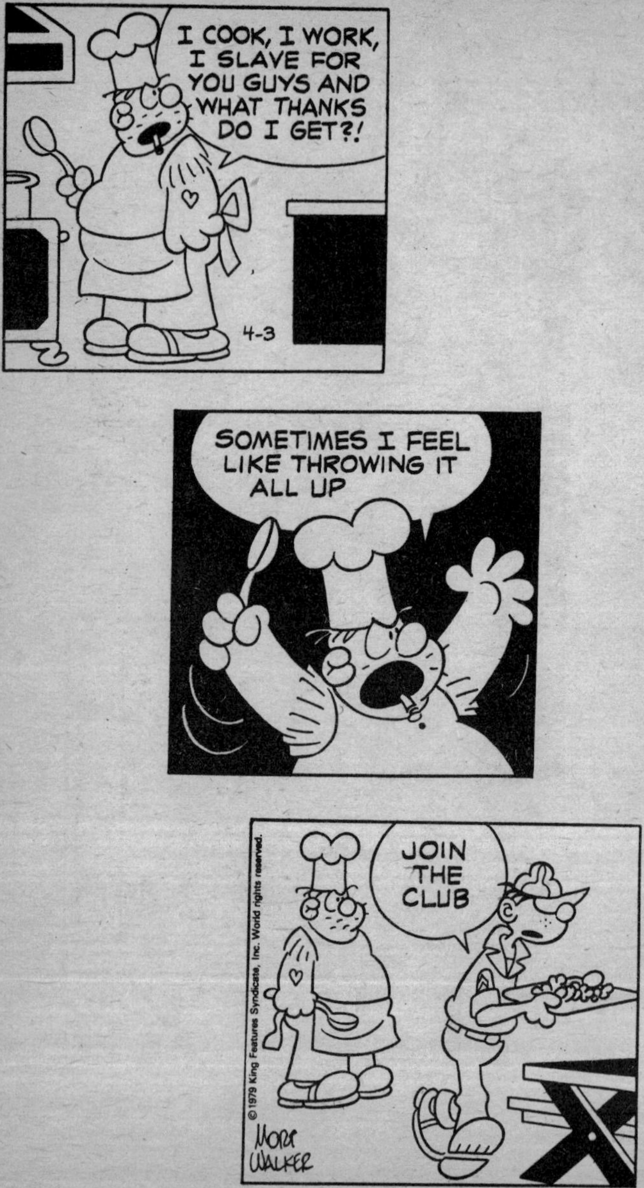
I COOK, I WORK, I SLAVE FOR YOU GUYS AND WHAT THANKS DO I GET?!
4-3
SOMETIMES I FEEL LIKE THROWING IT ALL UP
JOIN THE CLUB
© 1979 King Features Syndicate, Inc. World rights reserved.
MORT WALKER

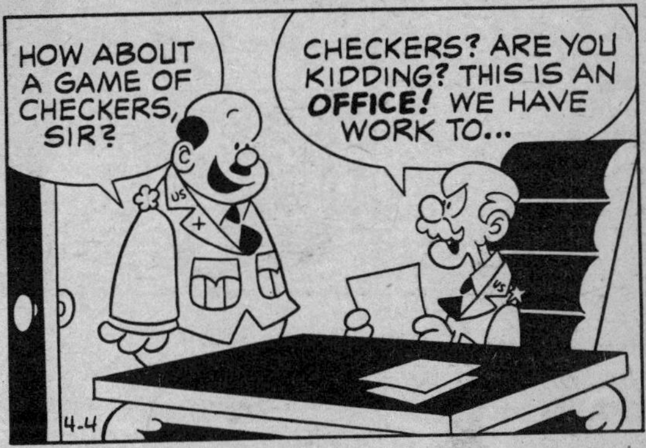
HOW ABOUT A GAME OF CHECKERS, SIR?
CHECKERS? ARE YOU KIDDING? THIS IS AN **OFFICE!** WE HAVE WORK TO...
4-4

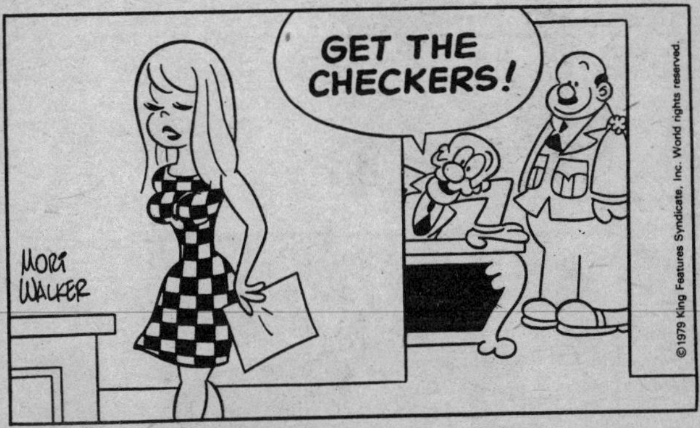
GET THE CHECKERS!
MORT WALKER

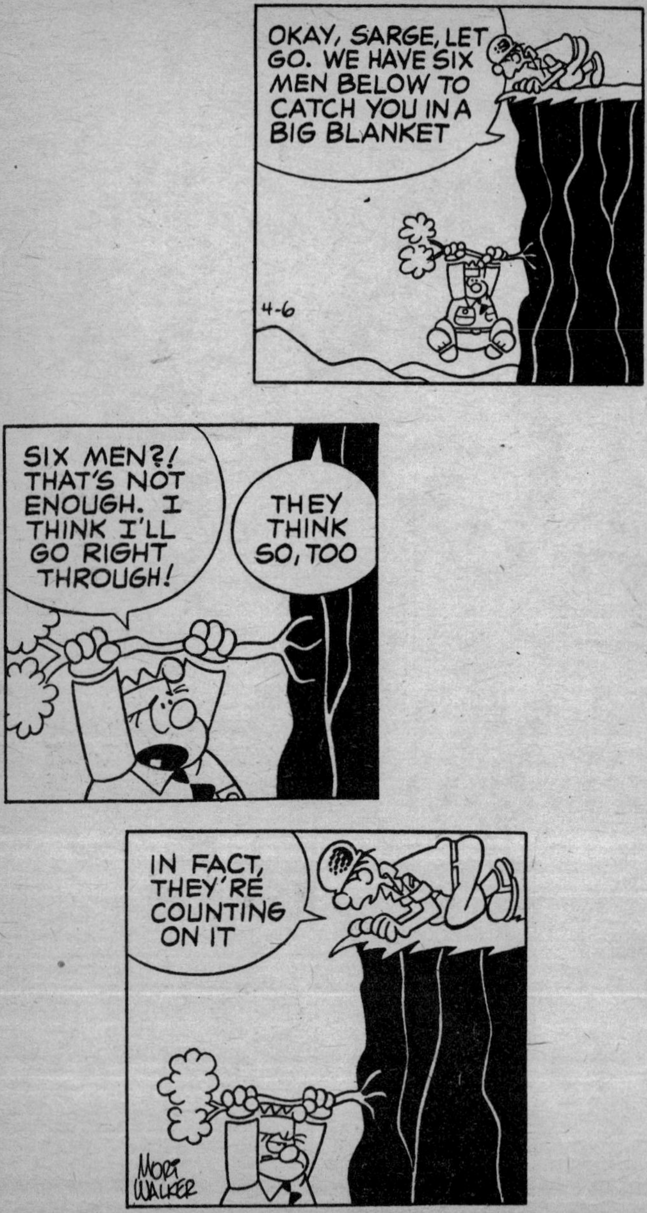
OKAY, SARGE, LET GO. WE HAVE SIX MEN BELOW TO CATCH YOU IN A BIG BLANKET
4-6
SIX MEN?! THAT'S NOT ENOUGH. I THINK I'LL GO RIGHT THROUGH!
THEY THINK SO, TOO
IN FACT, THEY'RE COUNTING ON IT
MORT WALKER

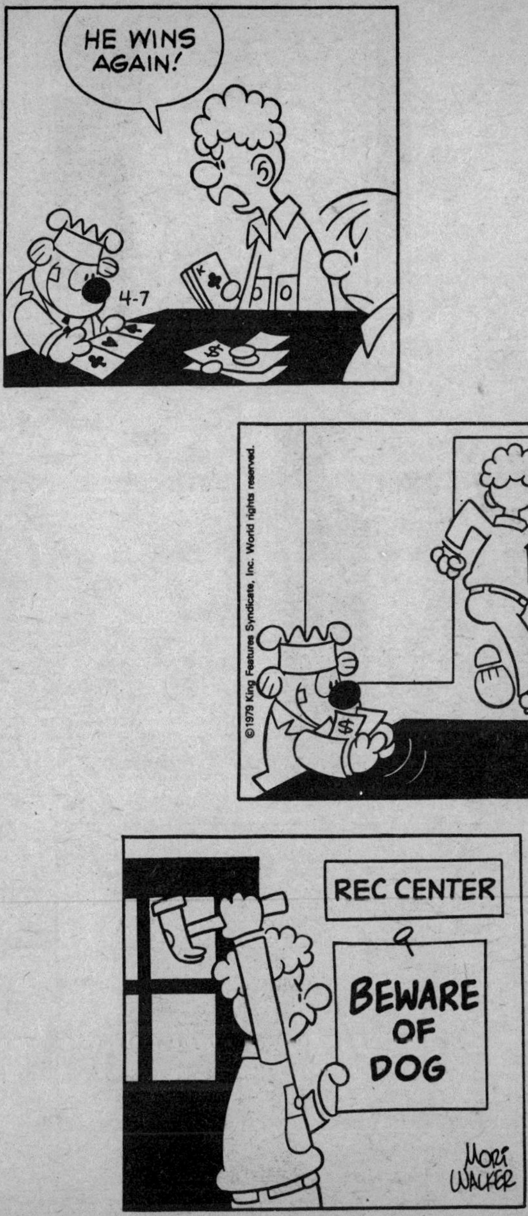
HE WINS AGAIN!
4-7
©1979 King Features Syndicate, Inc. World rights reserved.
REC CENTER
BEWARE OF DOG
MORT WALKER

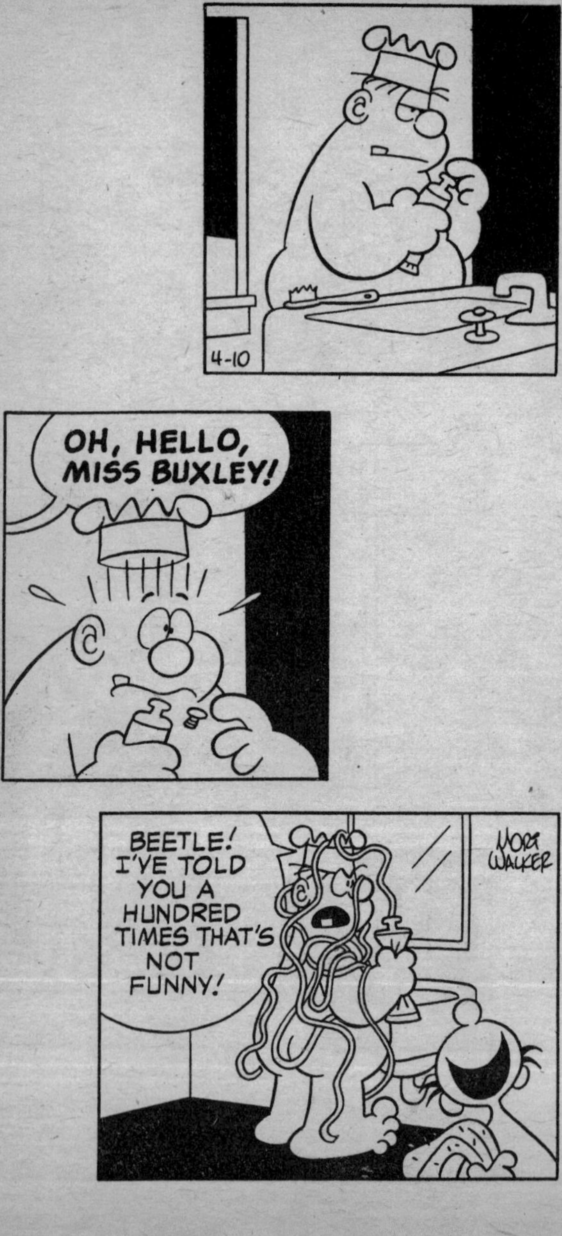
4-10
OH, HELLO, MISS BUXLEY!
BEETLE! I'VE TOLD YOU A HUNDRED TIMES THAT'S NOT FUNNY!
MORT WALKER

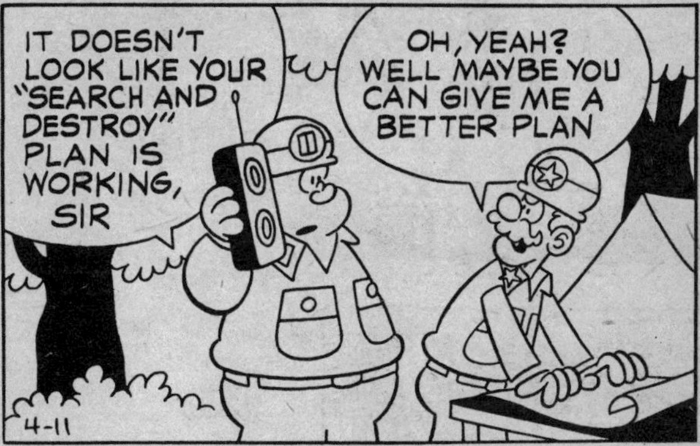
IT DOESN'T LOOK LIKE YOUR "SEARCH AND DESTROY" PLAN IS WORKING, SIR
OH, YEAH? WELL MAYBE YOU CAN GIVE ME A BETTER PLAN
4-11

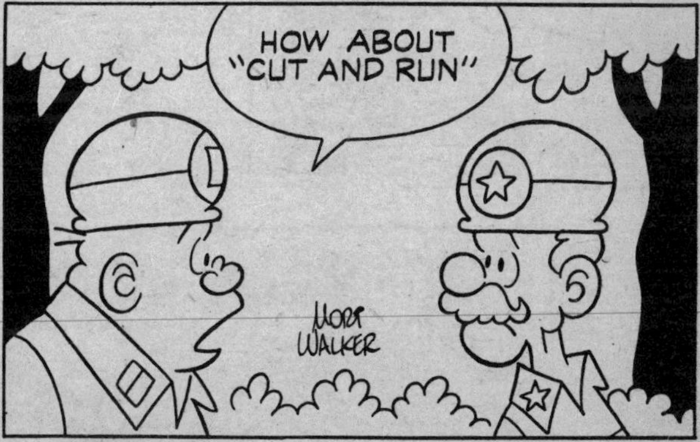
HOW ABOUT "CUT AND RUN"
MORT WALKER

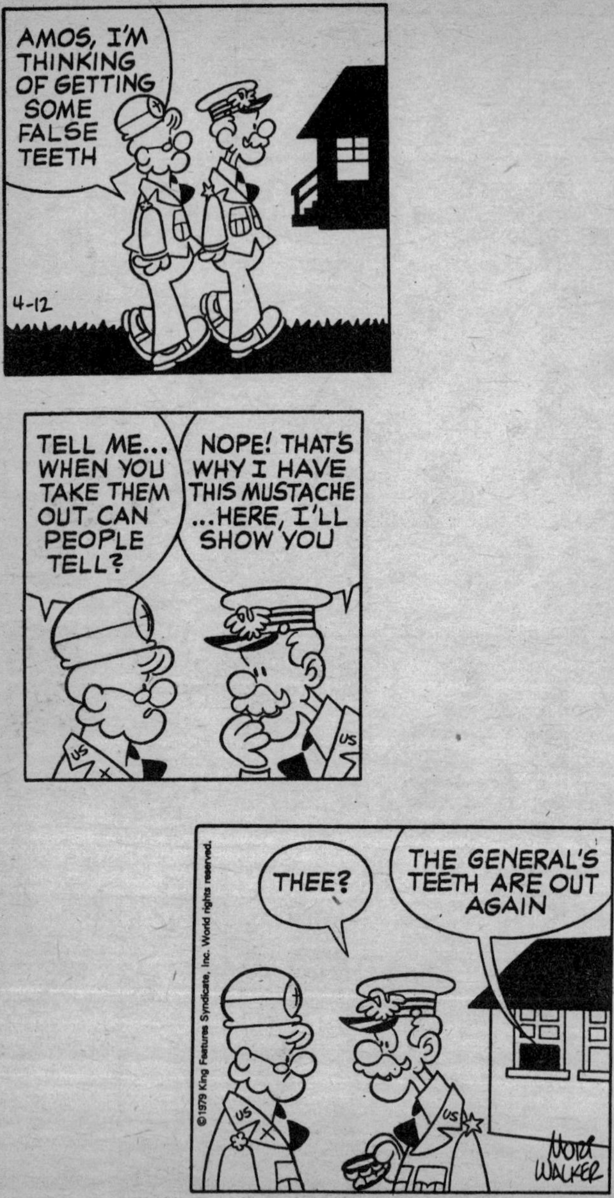
AMOS, I'M THINKING OF GETTING SOME FALSE TEETH
4-12
TELL ME... WHEN YOU TAKE THEM OUT CAN PEOPLE TELL?
NOPE! THAT'S WHY I HAVE THIS MUSTACHE ...HERE, I'LL SHOW YOU
THE GENERAL'S TEETH ARE OUT AGAIN
THEE?
©1979 King Features Syndicate, Inc. World rights reserved.
MORT WALKER

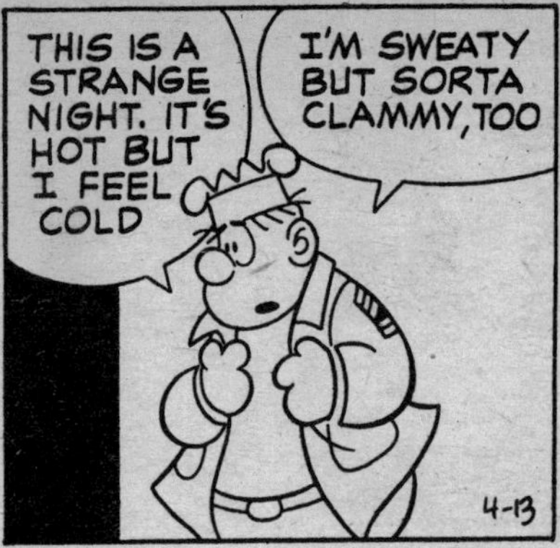
THIS IS A STRANGE NIGHT. IT'S HOT BUT I FEEL COLD
I'M SWEATY BUT SORTA CLAMMY, TOO
4-13

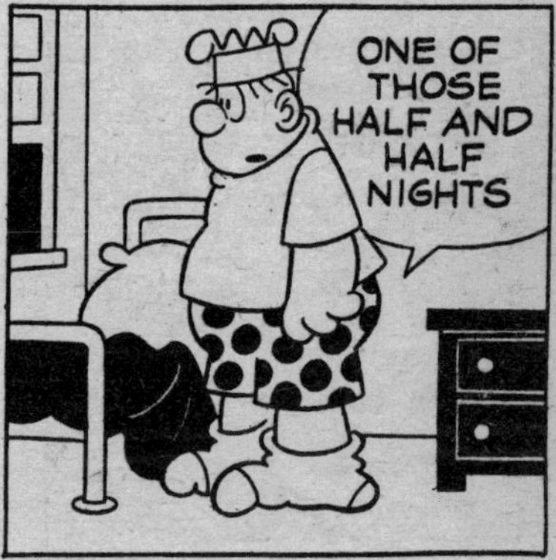
ONE OF THOSE HALF AND HALF NIGHTS

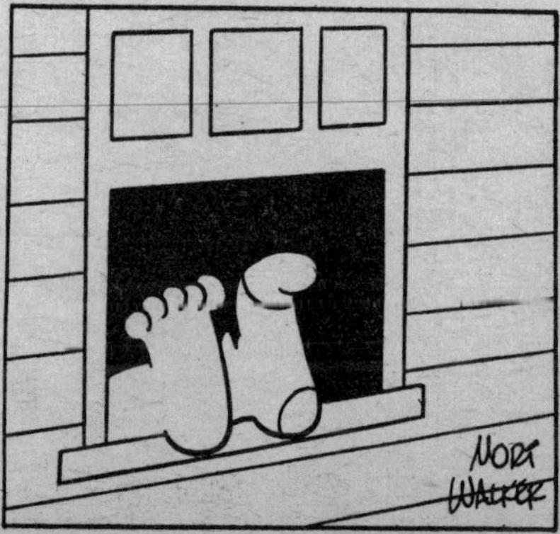
MORT WALKER

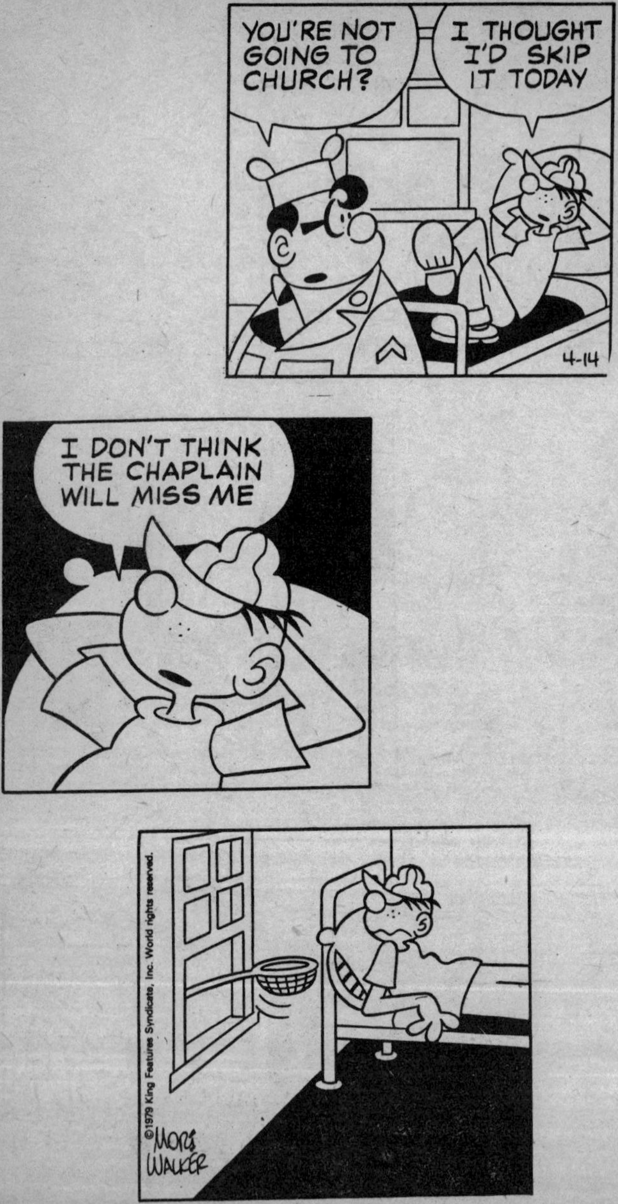
YOU'RE NOT GOING TO CHURCH?
I THOUGHT I'D SKIP IT TODAY
4-14
I DON'T THINK THE CHAPLAIN WILL MISS ME
©1979 King Features Syndicate, Inc. World rights reserved.
MORT WALKER

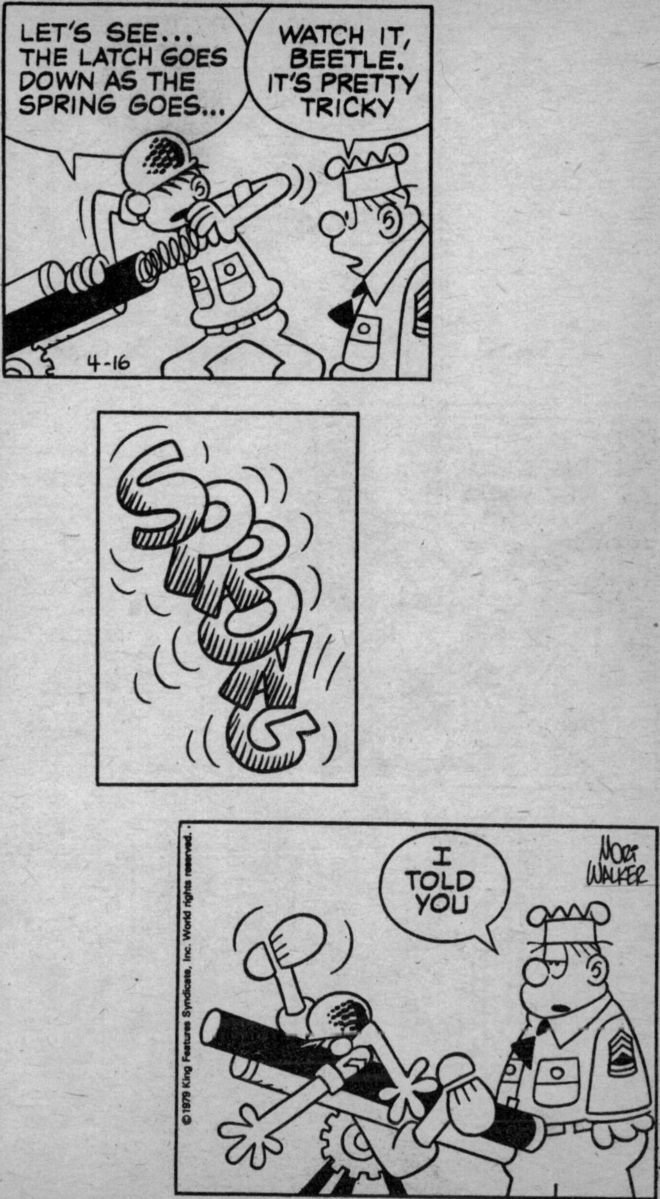
LET'S SEE... THE LATCH GOES DOWN AS THE SPRING GOES...
WATCH IT, BEETLE. IT'S PRETTY TRICKY
4-16
SPRONG
I TOLD YOU
MORT WALKER
©1979 King Features Syndicate, Inc. World rights reserved.

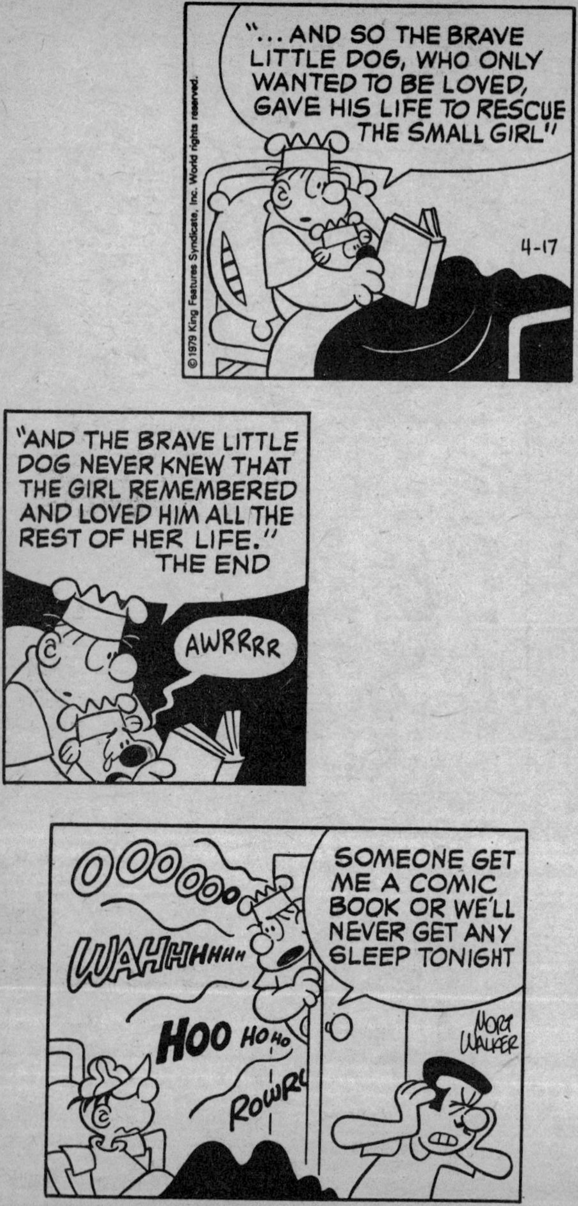
"...AND SO THE BRAVE LITTLE DOG, WHO ONLY WANTED TO BE LOVED, GAVE HIS LIFE TO RESCUE THE SMALL GIRL"
©1979 King Features Syndicate, Inc. World rights reserved.
4-17
"AND THE BRAVE LITTLE DOG NEVER KNEW THAT THE GIRL REMEMBERED AND LOVED HIM ALL THE REST OF HER LIFE." THE END
AWRRRR
OOOOOOO
WAHHHHHH
HOO HO HO
ROWR
SOMEONE GET ME A COMIC BOOK OR WE'LL NEVER GET ANY SLEEP TONIGHT
MORT WALKER

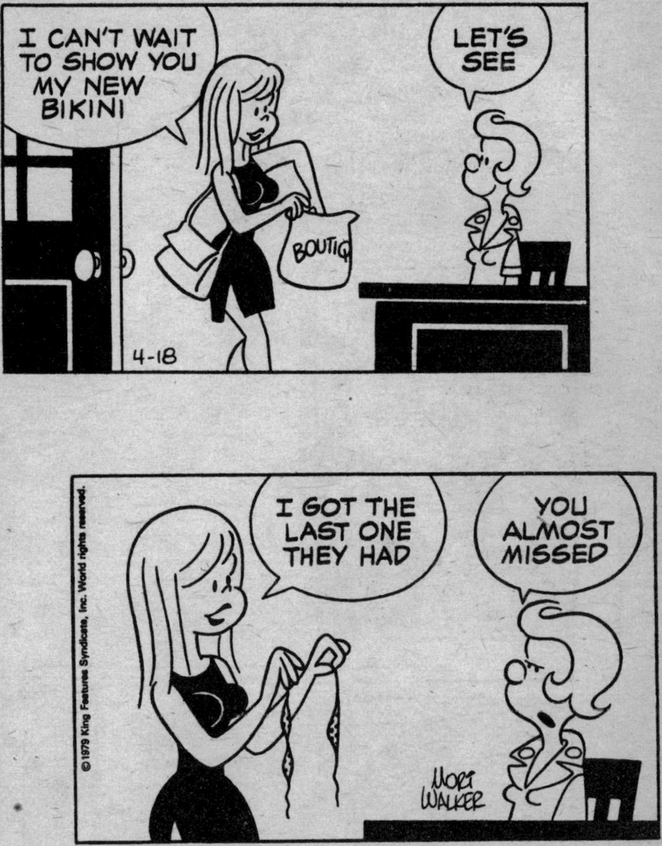
I CAN'T WAIT TO SHOW YOU MY NEW BIKINI
LET'S SEE
BOUTIQ
4-18
I GOT THE LAST ONE THEY HAD
YOU ALMOST MISSED
MORT WALKER
© 1979 King Features Syndicate, Inc. World rights reserved.

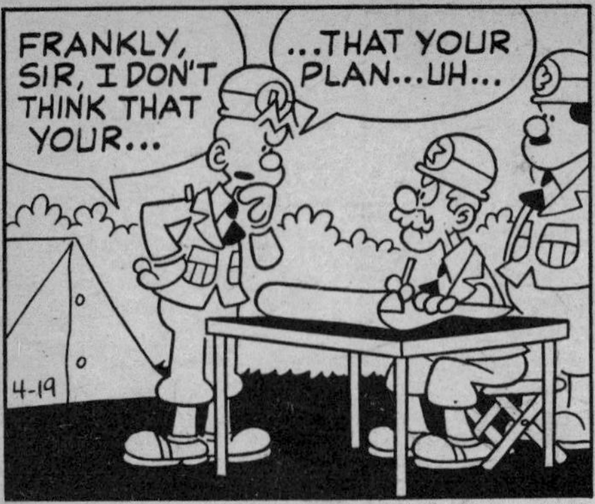
FRANKLY, SIR, I DON'T THINK THAT YOUR...
...THAT YOUR PLAN...UH...
4-19

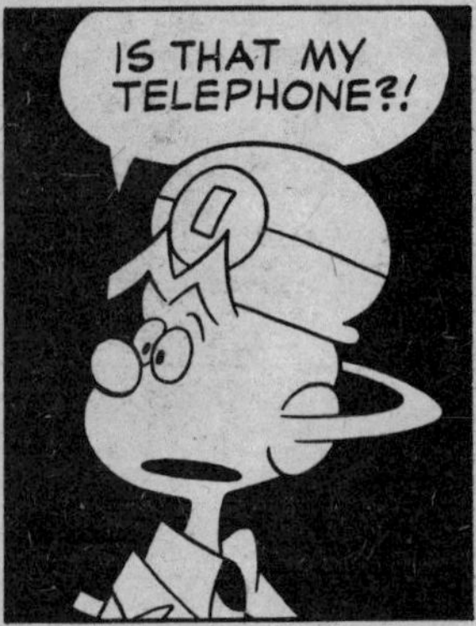
IS THAT MY TELEPHONE?!

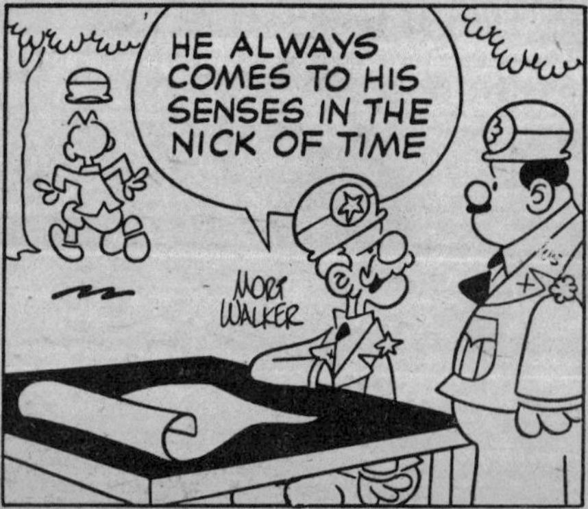
HE ALWAYS COMES TO HIS SENSES IN THE NICK OF TIME
MORT WALKER

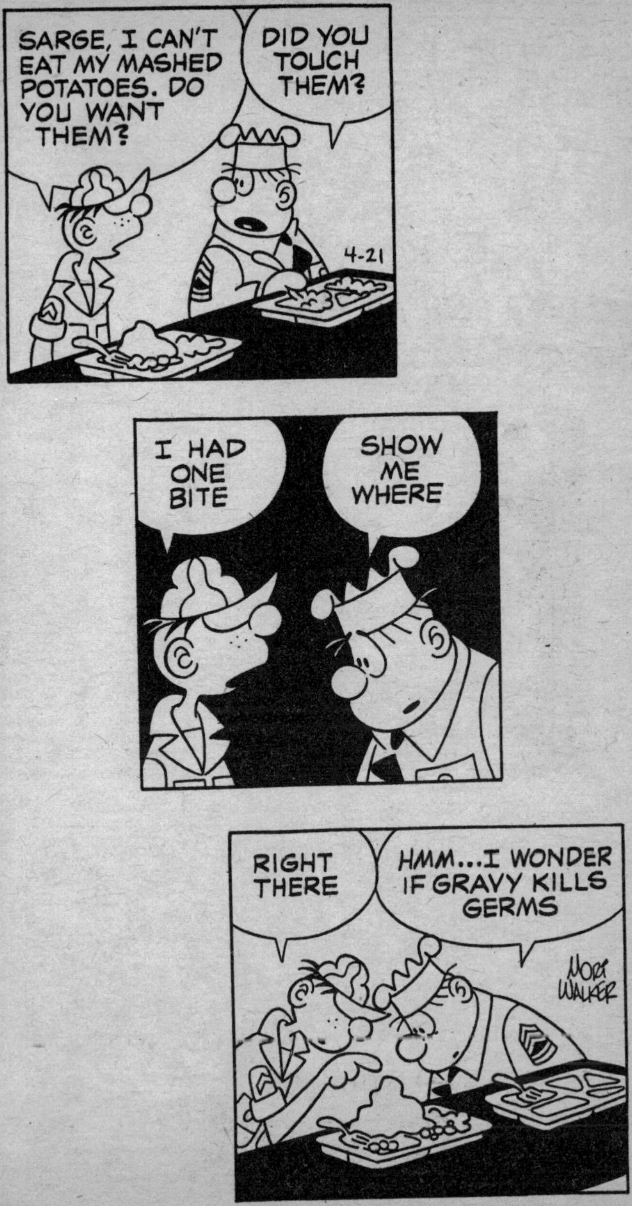
SARGE, I CAN'T EAT MY MASHED POTATOES. DO YOU WANT THEM?
DID YOU TOUCH THEM?
4-21
I HAD ONE BITE
SHOW ME WHERE
RIGHT THERE
HMM...I WONDER IF GRAVY KILLS GERMS
MORT WALKER

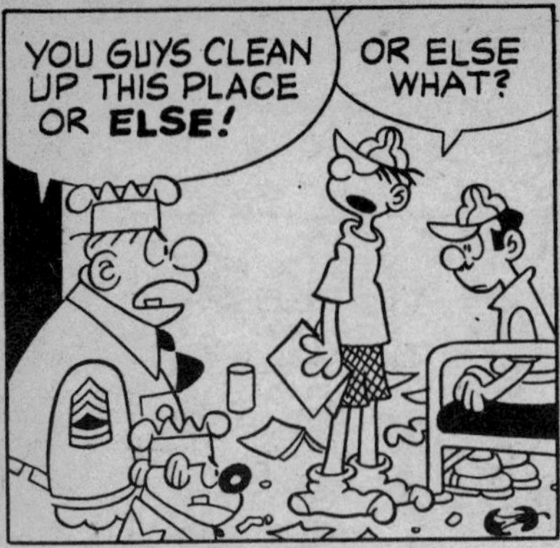
YOU GUYS CLEAN UP THIS PLACE OR **ELSE!**
OR ELSE WHAT?

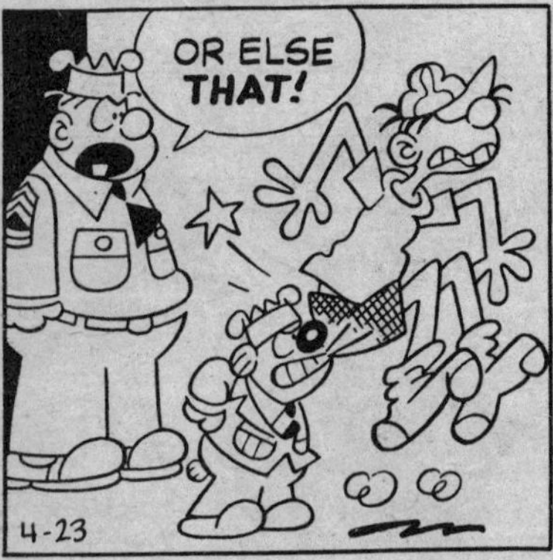
OR ELSE **THAT!**
4-23

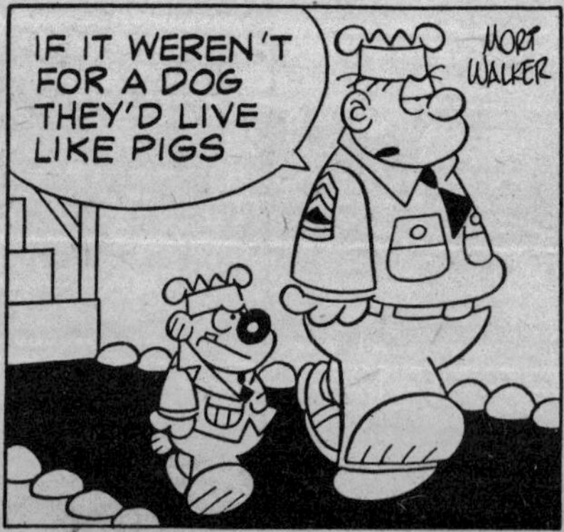
IF IT WEREN'T FOR A DOG THEY'D LIVE LIKE PIGS
MORT WALKER

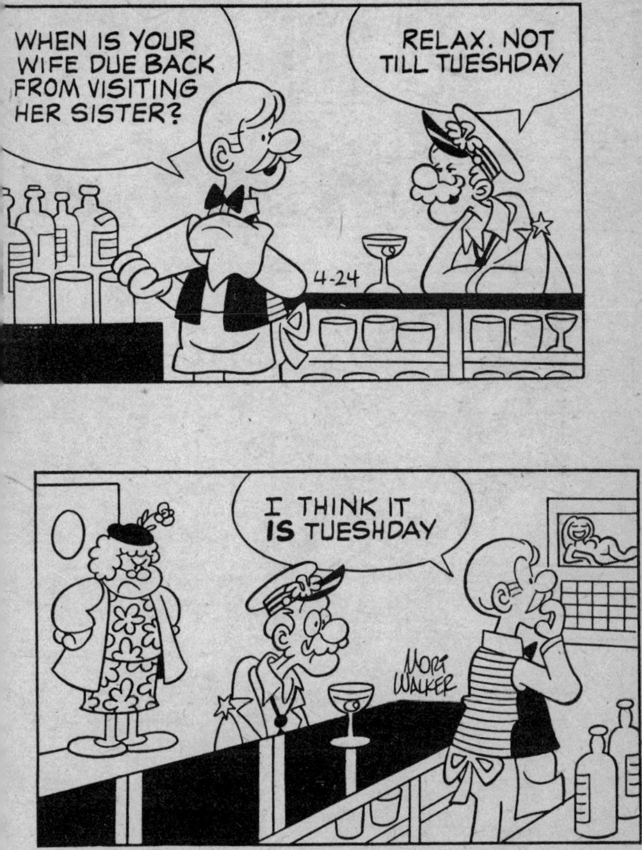
WHEN IS YOUR WIFE DUE BACK FROM VISITING HER SISTER?
RELAX. NOT TILL TUESHDAY
4-24
I THINK IT **IS** TUESHDAY
MORT WALKER

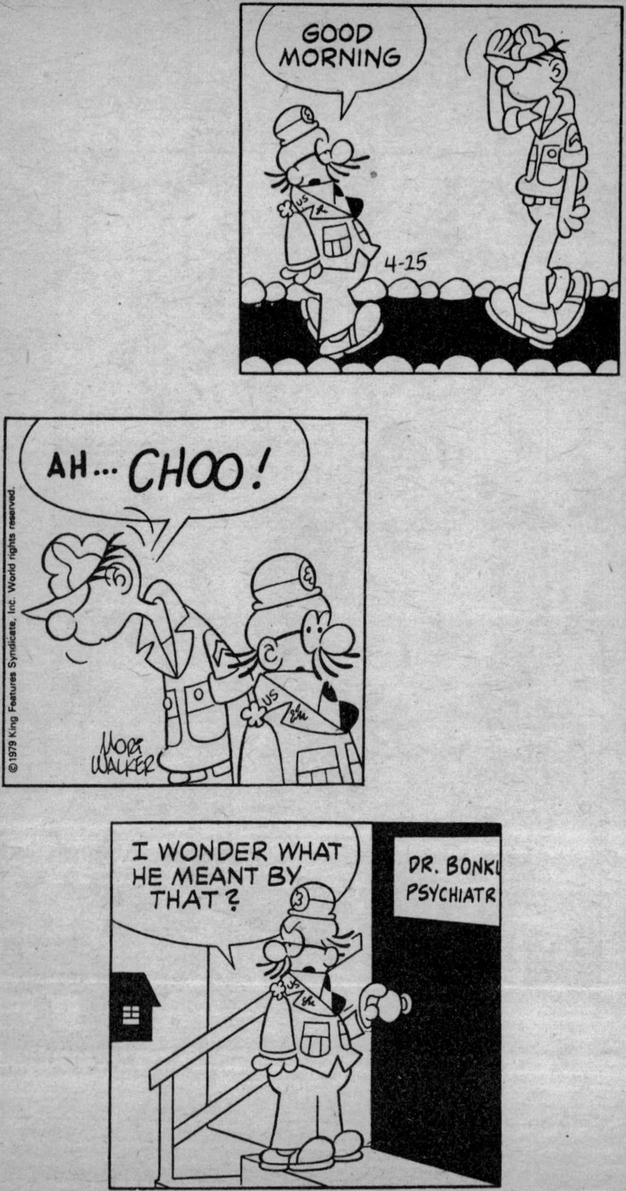
GOOD MORNING
4-25
AH... CHOO!
©1979 King Features Syndicate, Inc. World rights reserved.
MORT WALKER
I WONDER WHAT HE MEANT BY THAT?
DR. BONK
PSYCHIATR

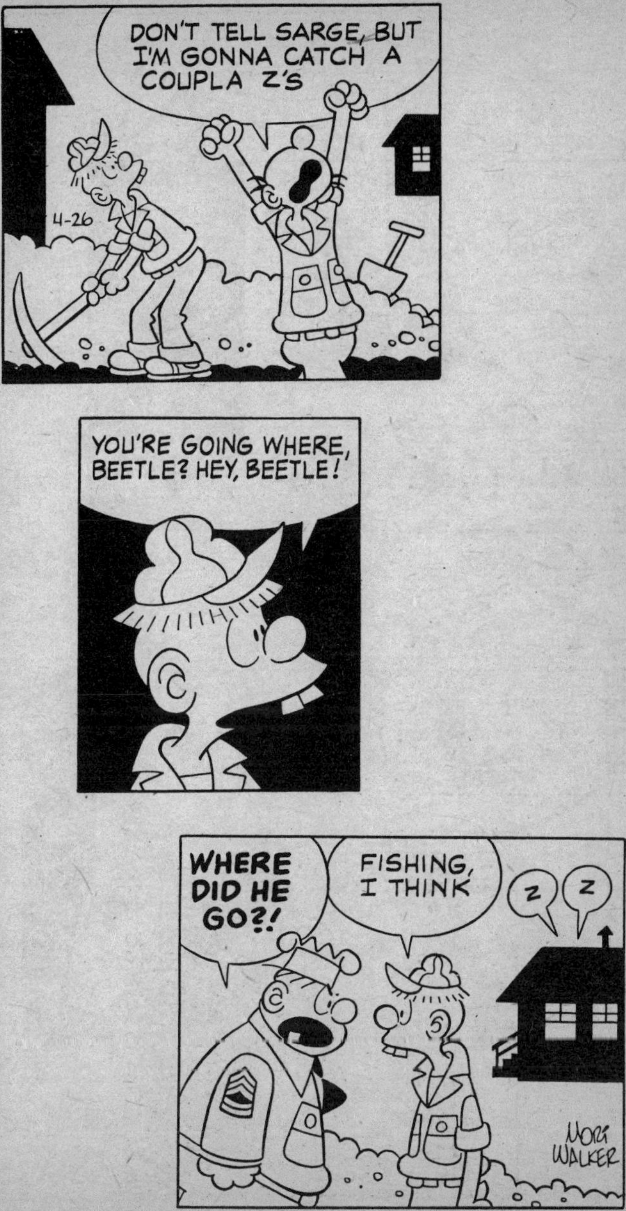
DON'T TELL SARGE, BUT I'M GONNA CATCH A COUPLA Z'S
4-26
YOU'RE GOING WHERE, BEETLE? HEY, BEETLE!
WHERE DID HE GO?!
FISHING, I THINK
Z
Z
MORT WALKER

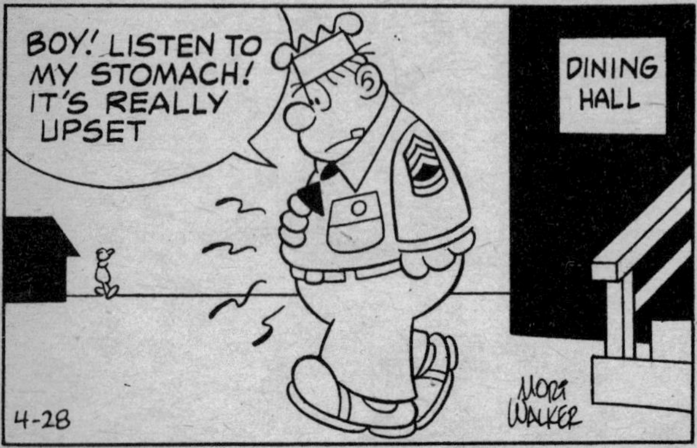
BOY! LISTEN TO MY STOMACH! IT'S REALLY UPSET
DINING HALL
4-28
MORT WALKER

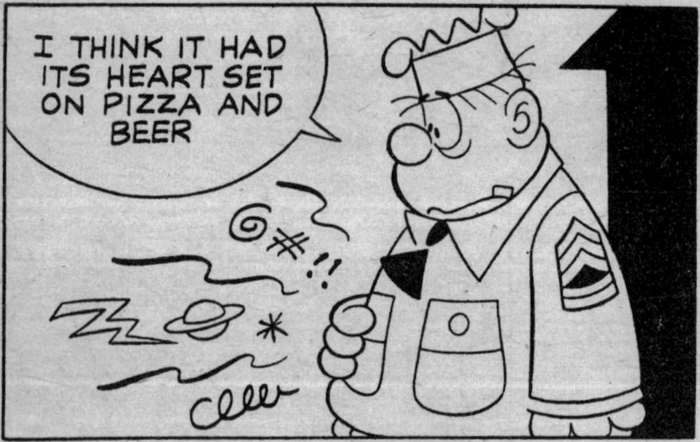
I THINK IT HAD ITS HEART SET ON PIZZA AND BEER

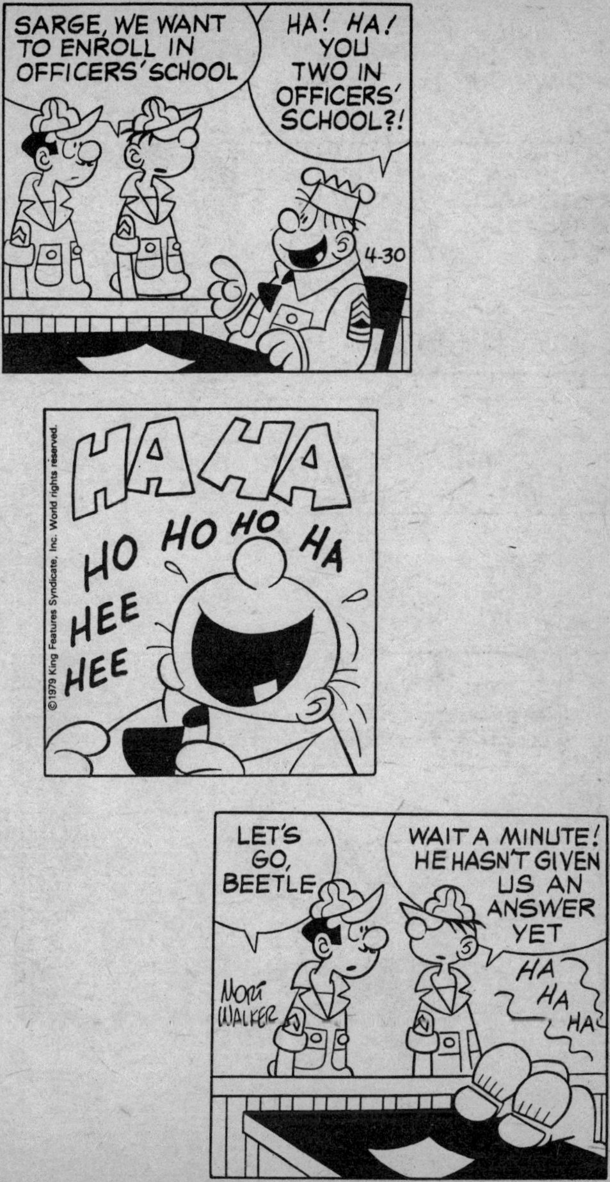
SARGE, WE WANT TO ENROLL IN OFFICERS' SCHOOL
HA! HA! YOU TWO IN OFFICERS' SCHOOL?!
4-30
HA HA
HO HO HO HA
HEE HEE
LET'S GO, BEETLE
WAIT A MINUTE! HE HASN'T GIVEN US AN ANSWER YET
HA HA HA
MORT WALKER

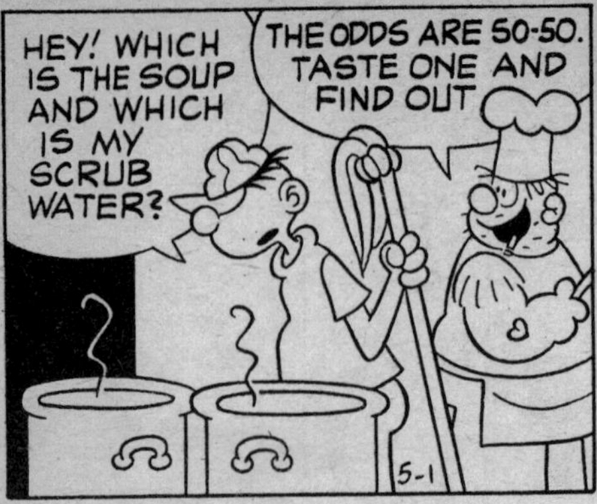
HEY! WHICH IS THE SOUP AND WHICH IS MY SCRUB WATER?
THE ODDS ARE 50-50. TASTE ONE AND FIND OUT
5-1

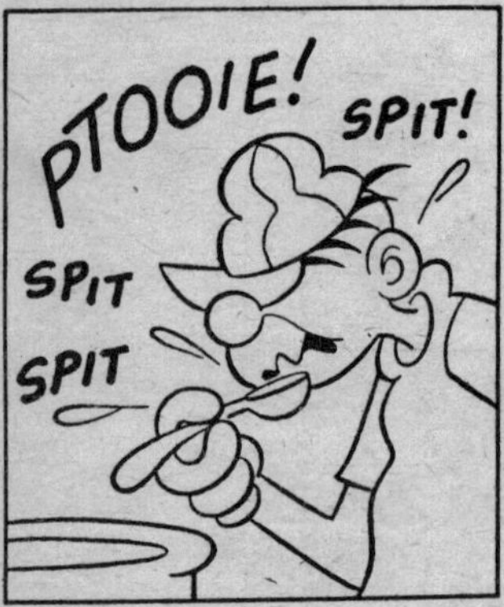
PTOOIE!
SPIT!
SPIT
SPIT

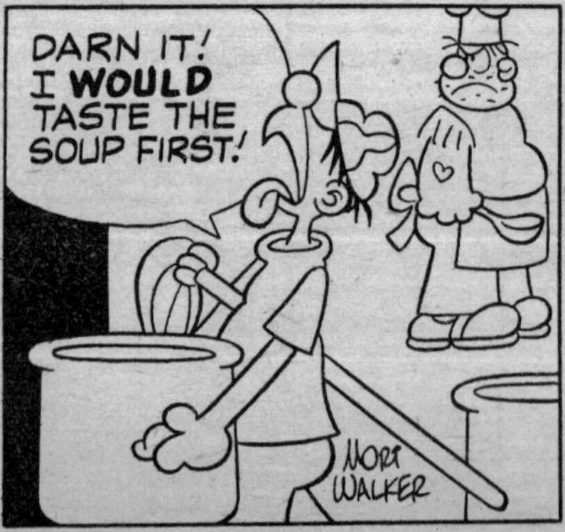
DARN IT! I **WOULD** TASTE THE SOUP FIRST!
MORT WALKER

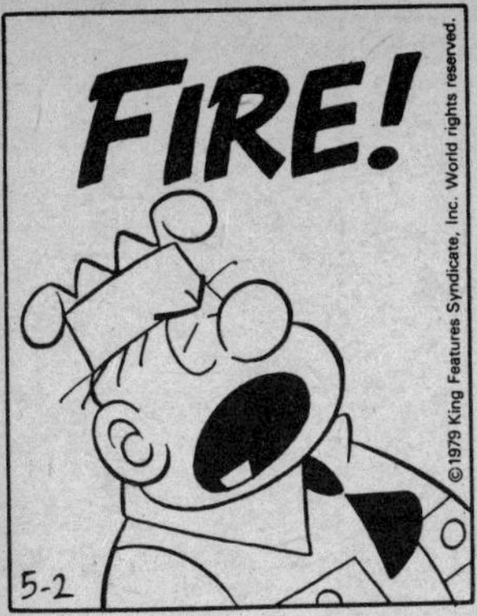
FIRE!
©1979 King Features Syndicate, Inc. World rights reserved.
5-2

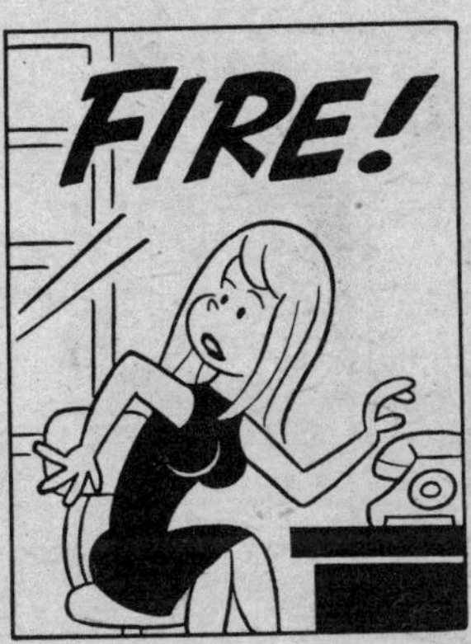
FIRE!

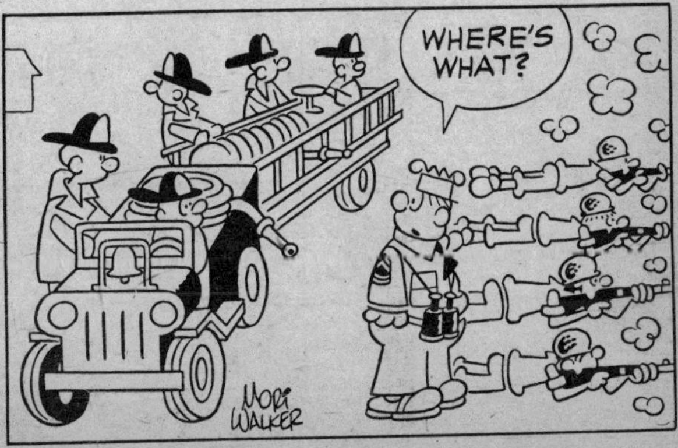
WHERE'S WHAT?
MORT WALKER

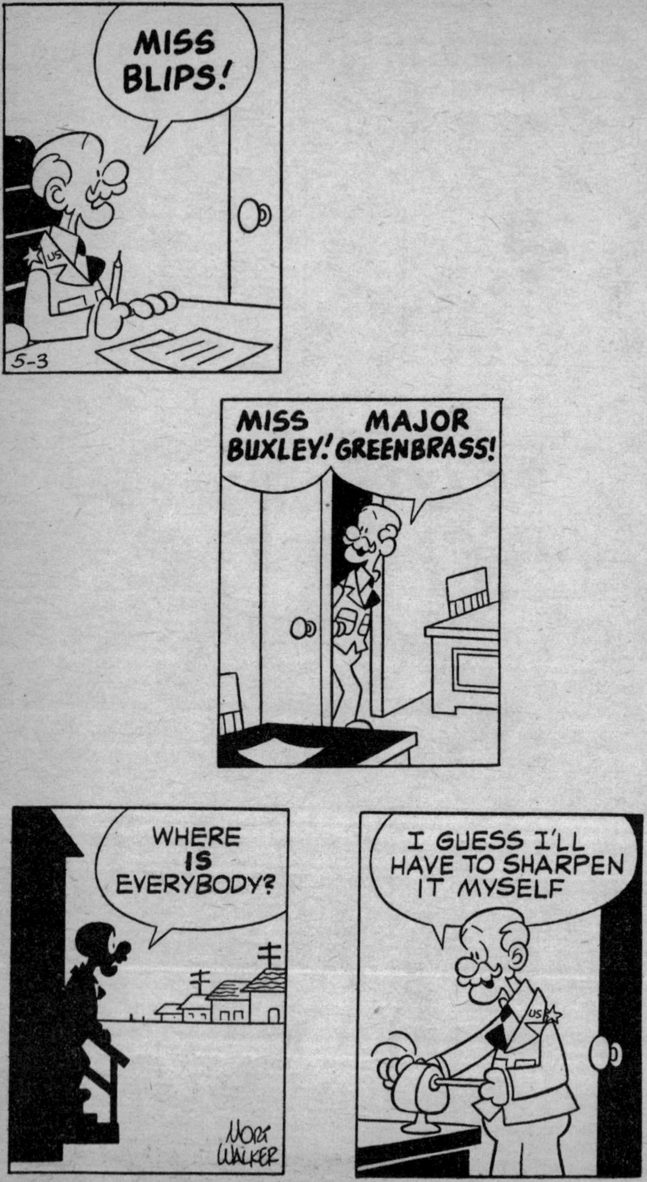
MISS BLIPS!
5-3
MISS BUXLEY!
MAJOR GREENBRASS!
WHERE IS EVERYBODY?
MORT WALKER
I GUESS I'LL HAVE TO SHARPEN IT MYSELF

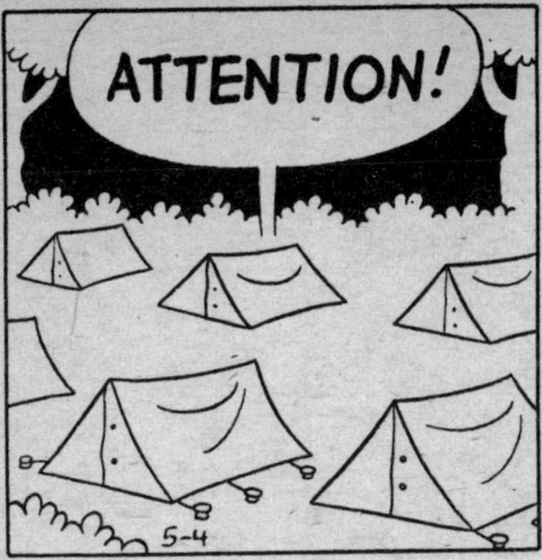
ATTENTION!
5-4

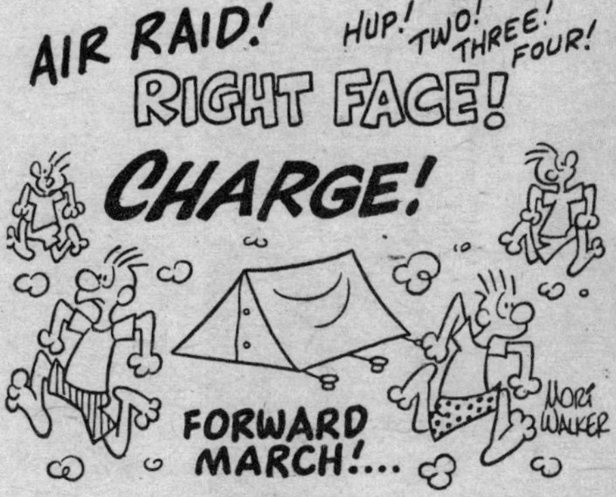
AIR RAID!
HUP! TWO! THREE! FOUR!
RIGHT FACE!
CHARGE!
FORWARD MARCH!...
MORT WALKER

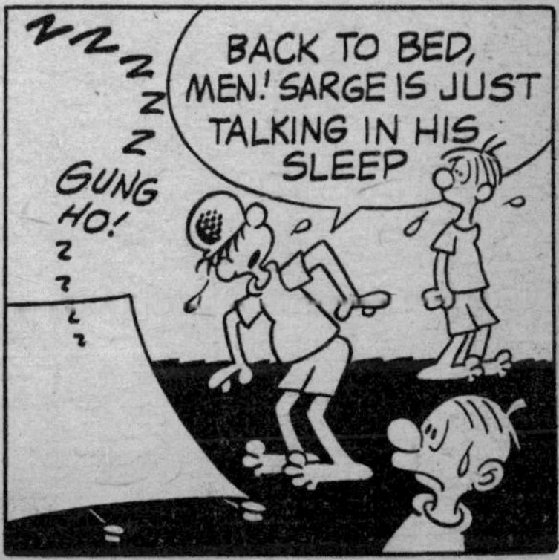
ZZZZZ
GUNG HO!
ZZZZ
BACK TO BED, MEN! SARGE IS JUST TALKING IN HIS SLEEP

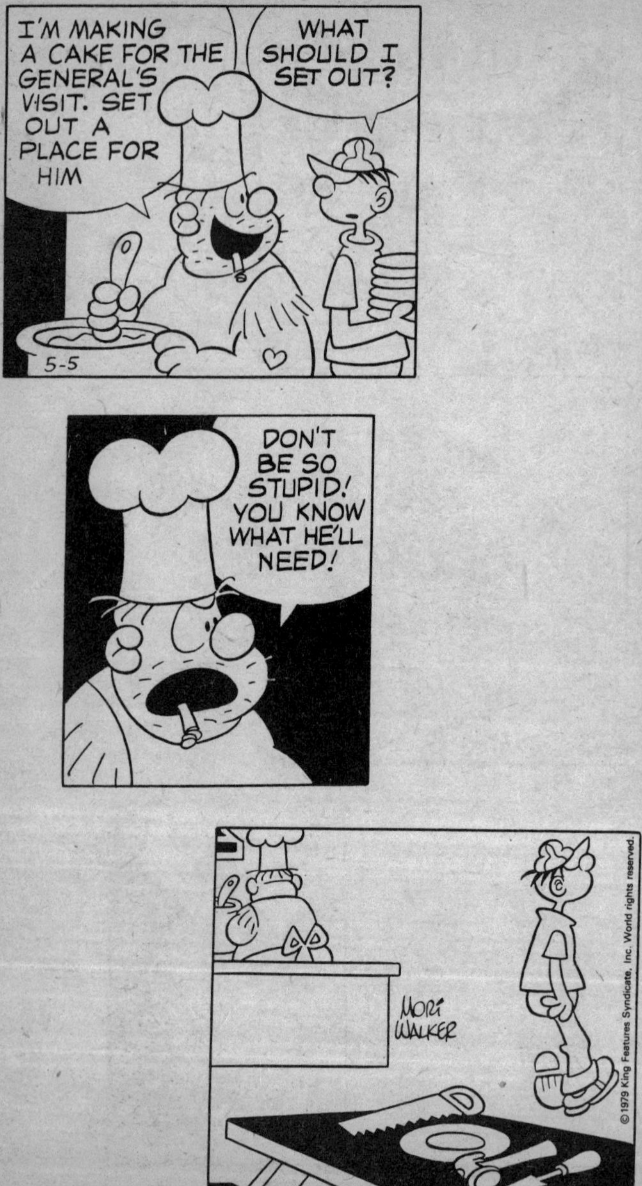
I'M MAKING A CAKE FOR THE GENERAL'S VISIT. SET OUT A PLACE FOR HIM
WHAT SHOULD I SET OUT?
5-5
DON'T BE SO STUPID! YOU KNOW WHAT HE'LL NEED!
MORT WALKER
© 1979 King Features Syndicate, Inc. World rights reserved.

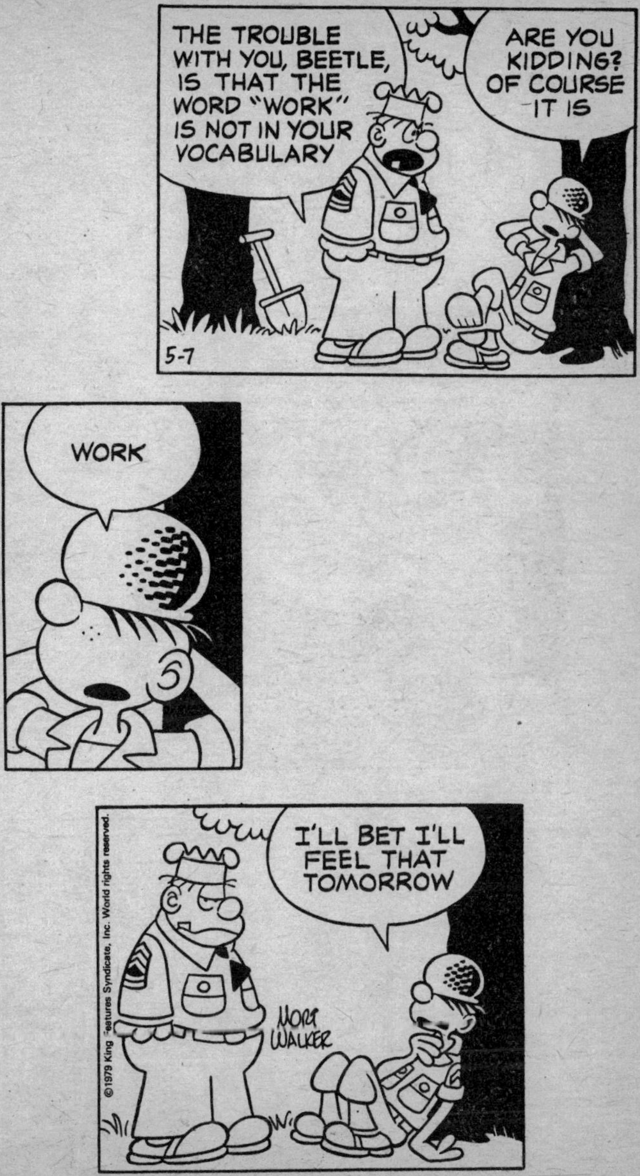
THE TROUBLE WITH YOU, BEETLE, IS THAT THE WORD "WORK" IS NOT IN YOUR VOCABULARY
ARE YOU KIDDING? OF COURSE IT IS
5-7
WORK
I'LL BET I'LL FEEL THAT TOMORROW
MORT WALKER

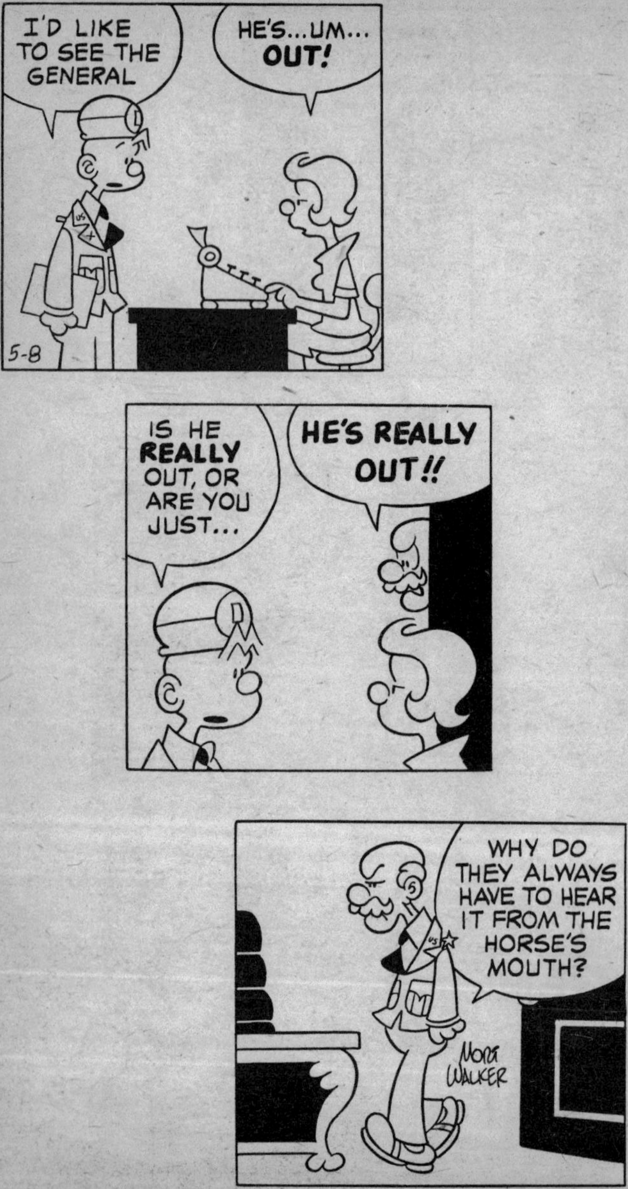
I'D LIKE TO SEE THE GENERAL
HE'S...UM... **OUT!**
5-8
IS HE **REALLY** OUT, OR ARE YOU JUST...
HE'S REALLY OUT!!
WHY DO THEY ALWAYS HAVE TO HEAR IT FROM THE HORSE'S MOUTH?
MORT WALKER

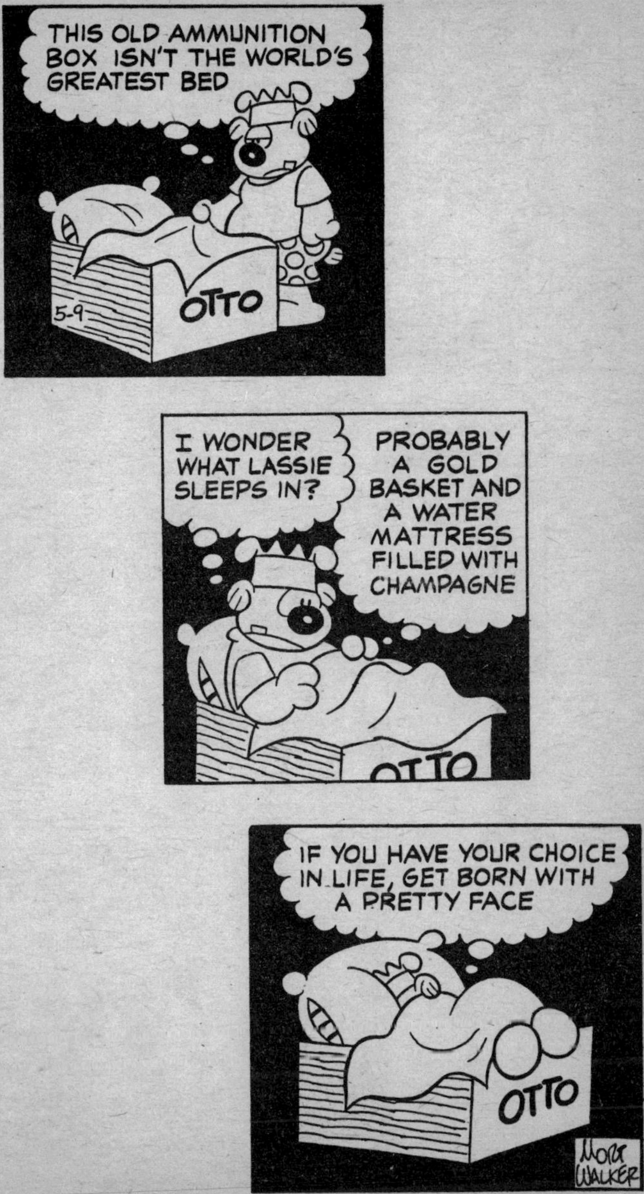
THIS OLD AMMUNITION BOX ISN'T THE WORLD'S GREATEST BED
OTTO
5-9
I WONDER WHAT LASSIE SLEEPS IN?
PROBABLY A GOLD BASKET AND A WATER MATTRESS FILLED WITH CHAMPAGNE
IF YOU HAVE YOUR CHOICE IN LIFE, GET BORN WITH A PRETTY FACE
OTTO
MORT WALKER

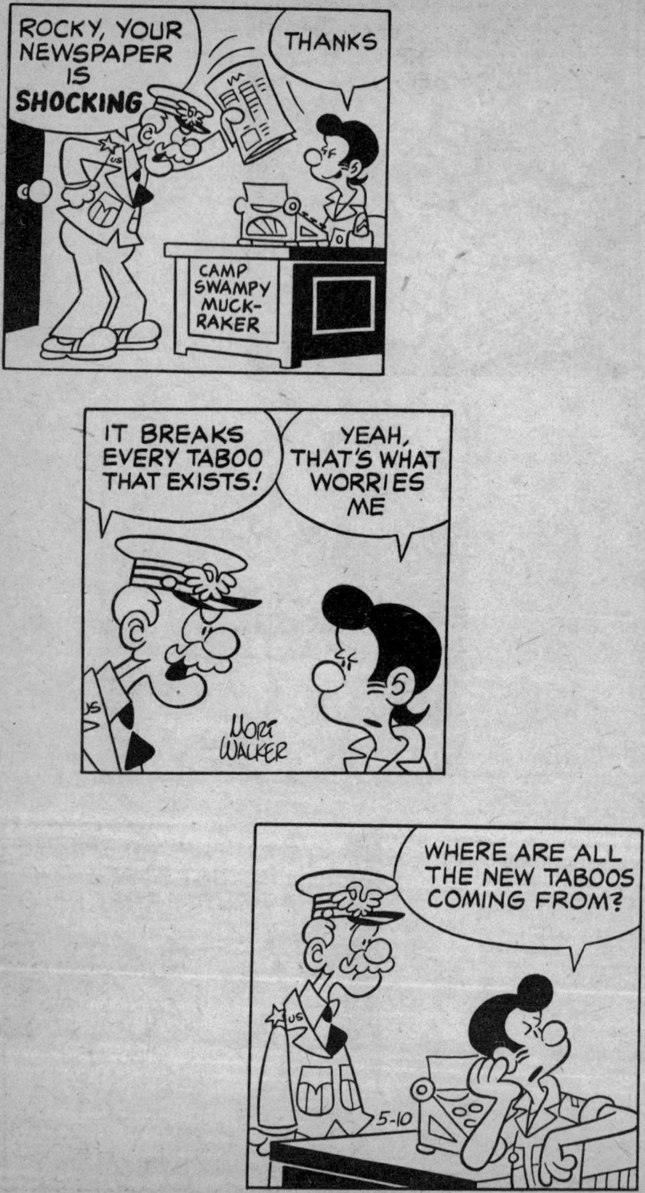
ROCKY, YOUR NEWSPAPER IS **SHOCKING**
THANKS
CAMP SWAMPY MUCK-RAKER
IT BREAKS EVERY TABOO THAT EXISTS!
YEAH, THAT'S WHAT WORRIES ME
MORT WALKER
WHERE ARE ALL THE NEW TABOOS COMING FROM?
5-10

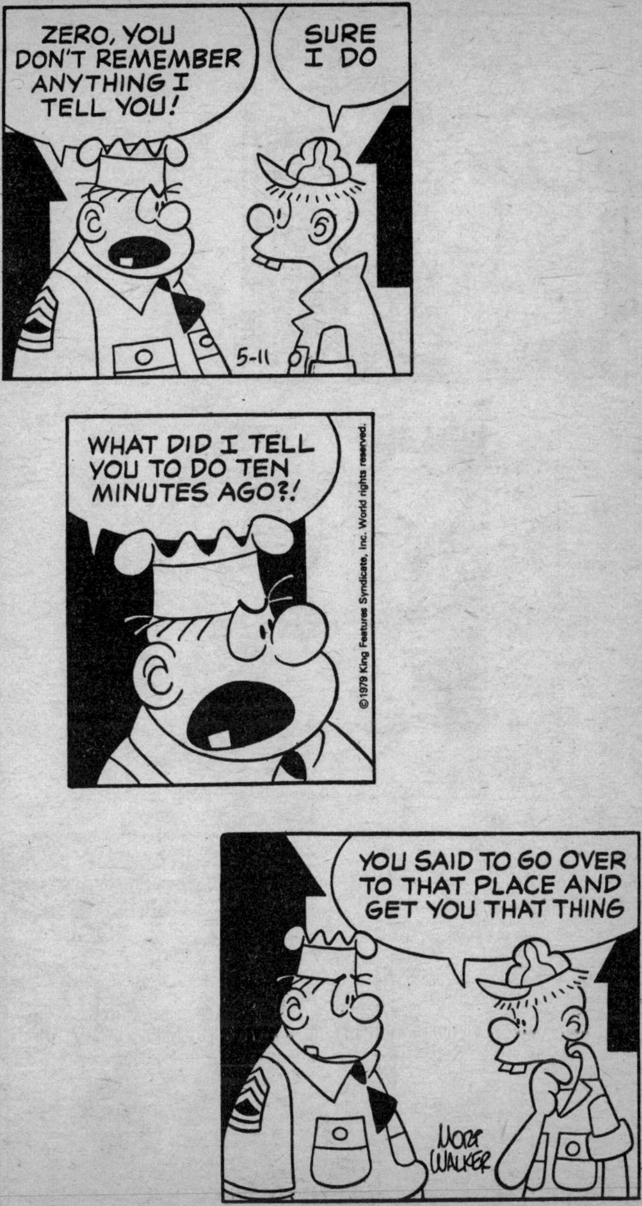
ZERO, YOU DON'T REMEMBER ANYTHING I TELL YOU!
SURE I DO
5-11
WHAT DID I TELL YOU TO DO TEN MINUTES AGO?!
YOU SAID TO GO OVER TO THAT PLACE AND GET YOU THAT THING
MORT WALKER

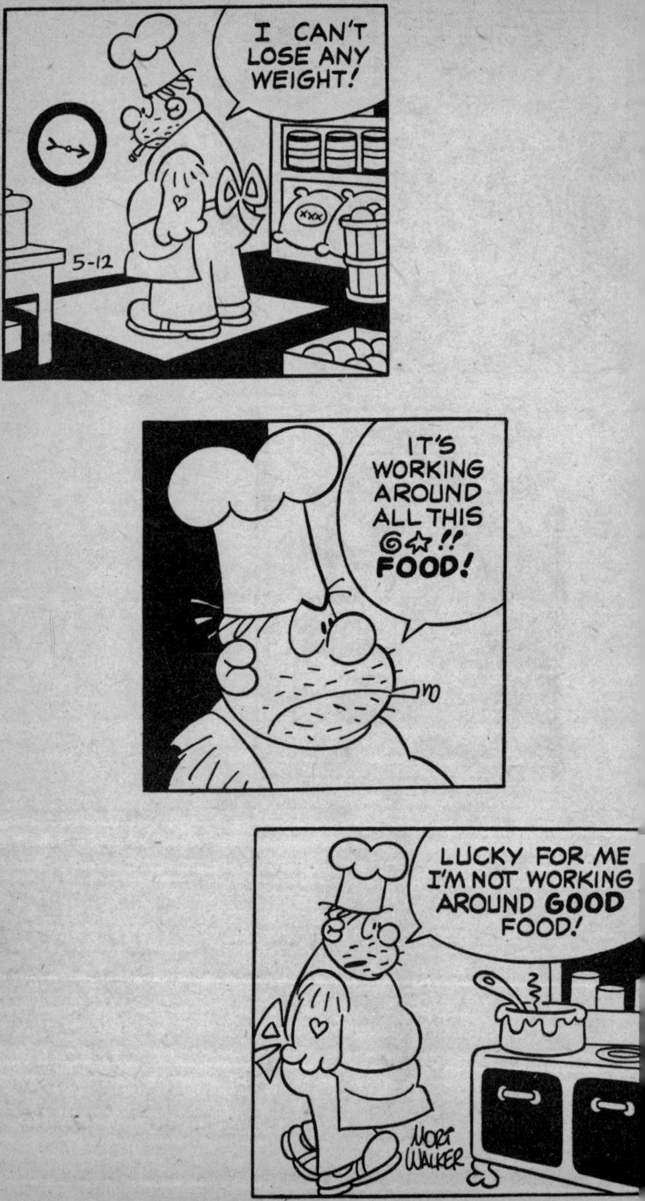
I CAN'T LOSE ANY WEIGHT!
5-12
IT'S WORKING AROUND ALL THIS @☆!! FOOD!
LUCKY FOR ME I'M NOT WORKING AROUND GOOD FOOD!
MORT WALKER

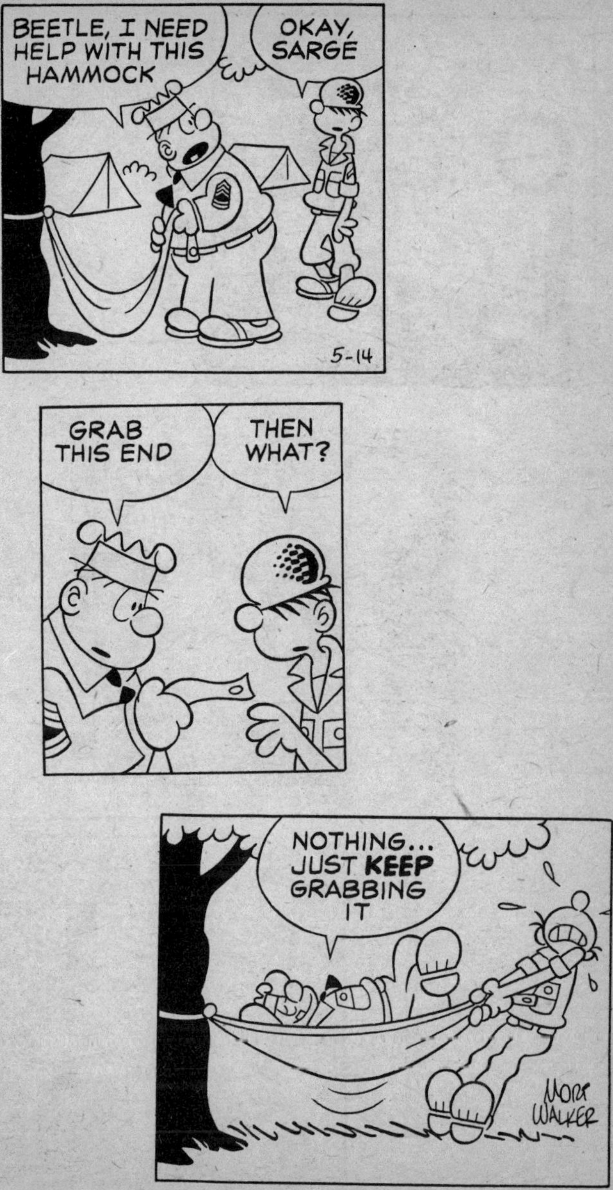
BEETLE, I NEED HELP WITH THIS HAMMOCK
OKAY, SARGE
5-14
GRAB THIS END
THEN WHAT?
NOTHING... JUST **KEEP** GRABBING IT
MORT WALKER

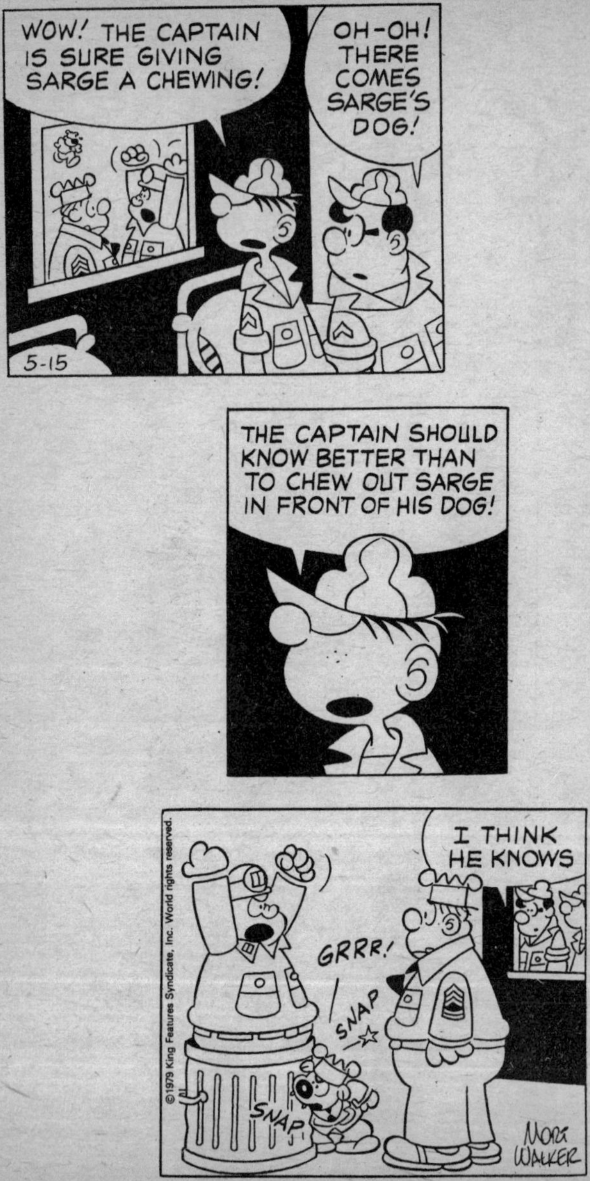
WOW! THE CAPTAIN IS SURE GIVING SARGE A CHEWING!
OH-OH! THERE COMES SARGE'S DOG!
5-15
THE CAPTAIN SHOULD KNOW BETTER THAN TO CHEW OUT SARGE IN FRONT OF HIS DOG!
©1979 King Features Syndicate, Inc. World rights reserved.
I THINK HE KNOWS
GRRR!
SNAP
SNAP
MORT WALKER

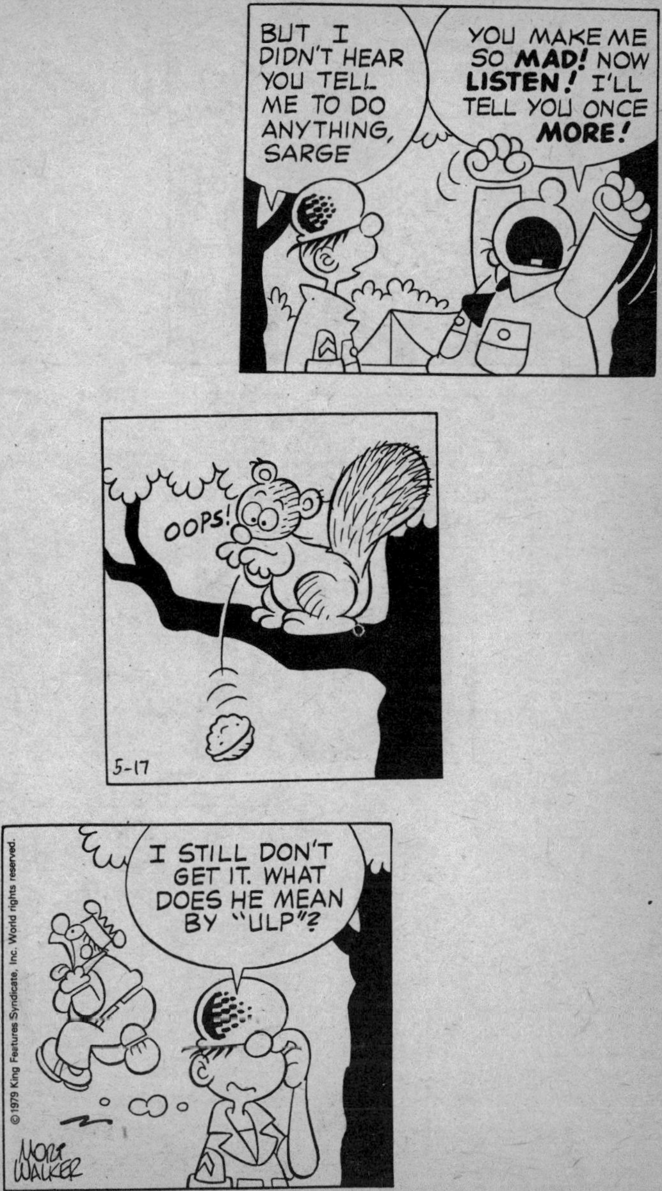
BUT I DIDN'T HEAR YOU TELL ME TO DO ANYTHING, SARGE
YOU MAKE ME SO **MAD!** NOW **LISTEN!** I'LL TELL YOU ONCE **MORE!**
OOPS!
5-17
I STILL DON'T GET IT. WHAT DOES HE MEAN BY "ULP"?
© 1979 King Features Syndicate, Inc. World rights reserved.
MORT WALKER

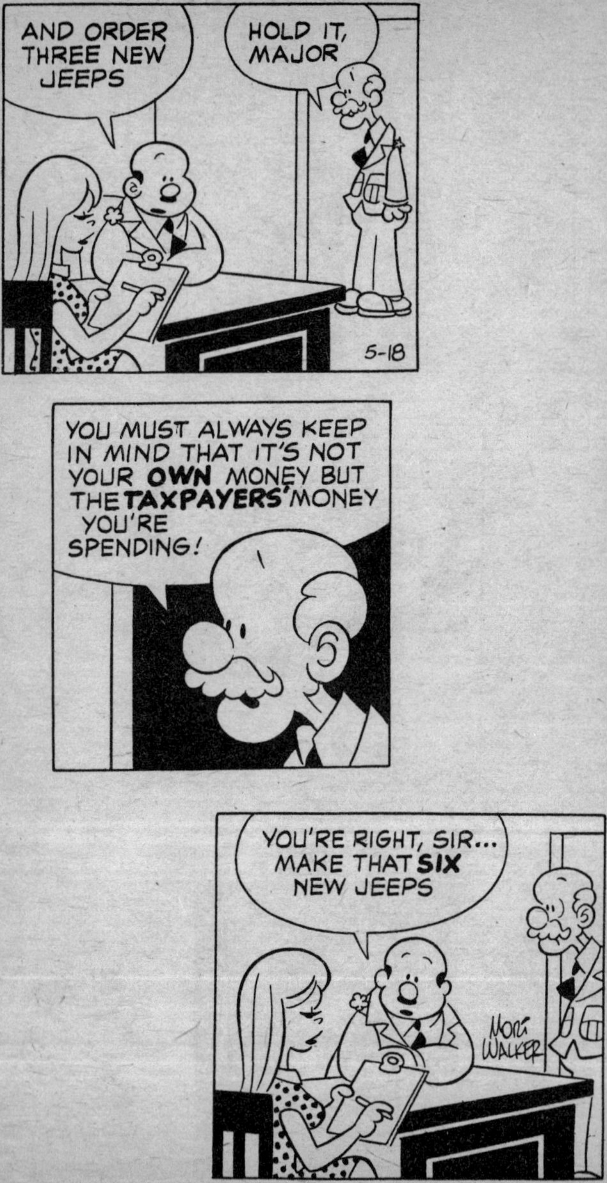
AND ORDER THREE NEW JEEPS
HOLD IT, MAJOR
5-18
YOU MUST ALWAYS KEEP IN MIND THAT IT'S NOT YOUR **OWN** MONEY BUT THE **TAXPAYERS'** MONEY YOU'RE SPENDING!
YOU'RE RIGHT, SIR... MAKE THAT **SIX** NEW JEEPS
MORT WALKER

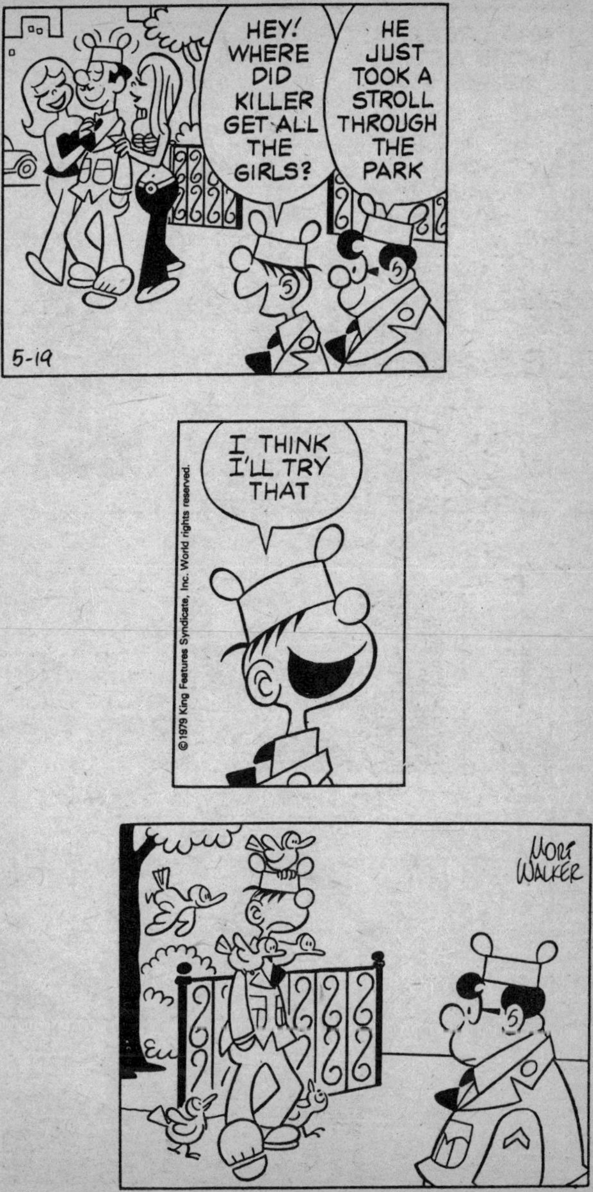

HEY! WHERE DID KILLER GET ALL THE GIRLS?
HE JUST TOOK A STROLL THROUGH THE PARK
5-19
I THINK I'LL TRY THAT
©1979 King Features Syndicate, Inc. World rights reserved.
MORT WALKER

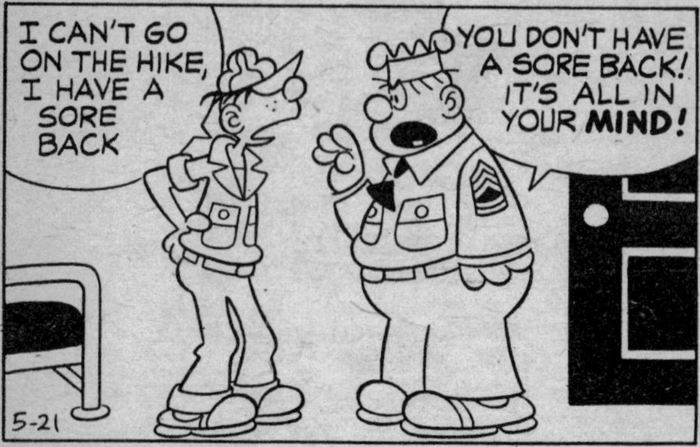
I CAN'T GO ON THE HIKE, I HAVE A SORE BACK
YOU DON'T HAVE A SORE BACK! IT'S ALL IN YOUR **MIND**!
5-21

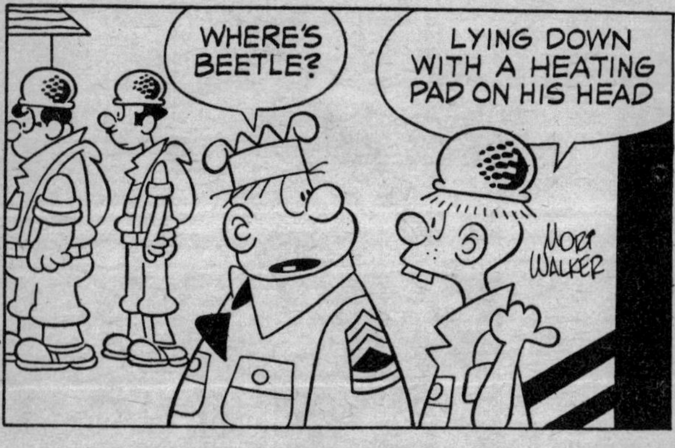
WHERE'S BEETLE?
LYING DOWN WITH A HEATING PAD ON HIS HEAD
MORT WALKER

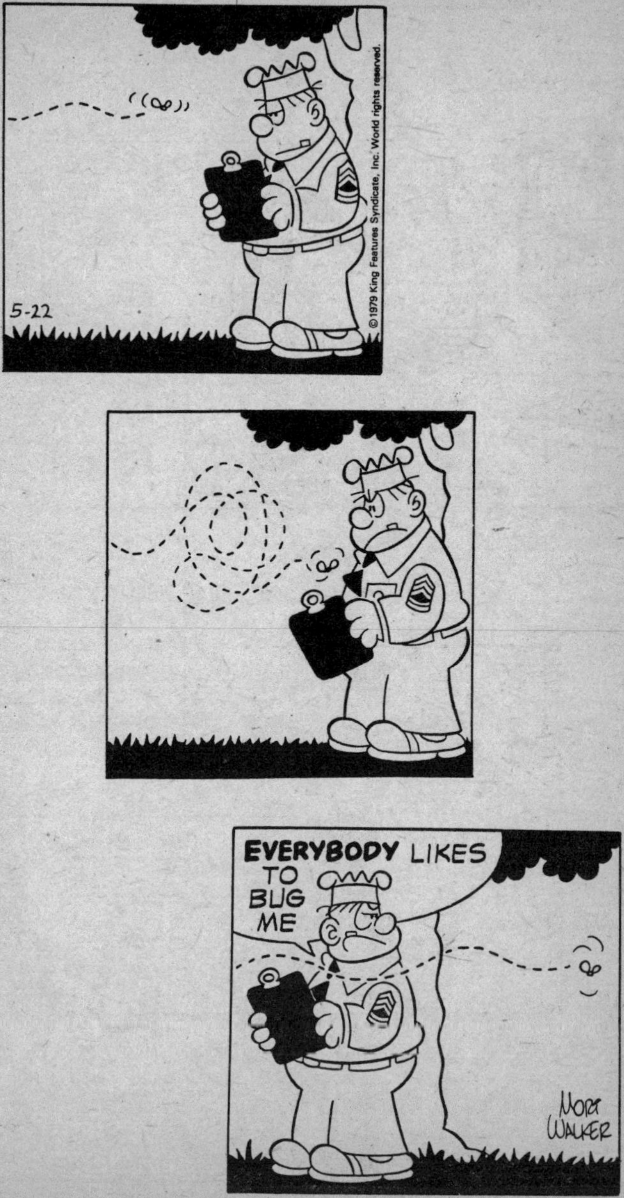
© 1979 King Features Syndicate, Inc. World rights reserved.
5-22
EVERYBODY LIKES TO BUG ME
MORT WALKER

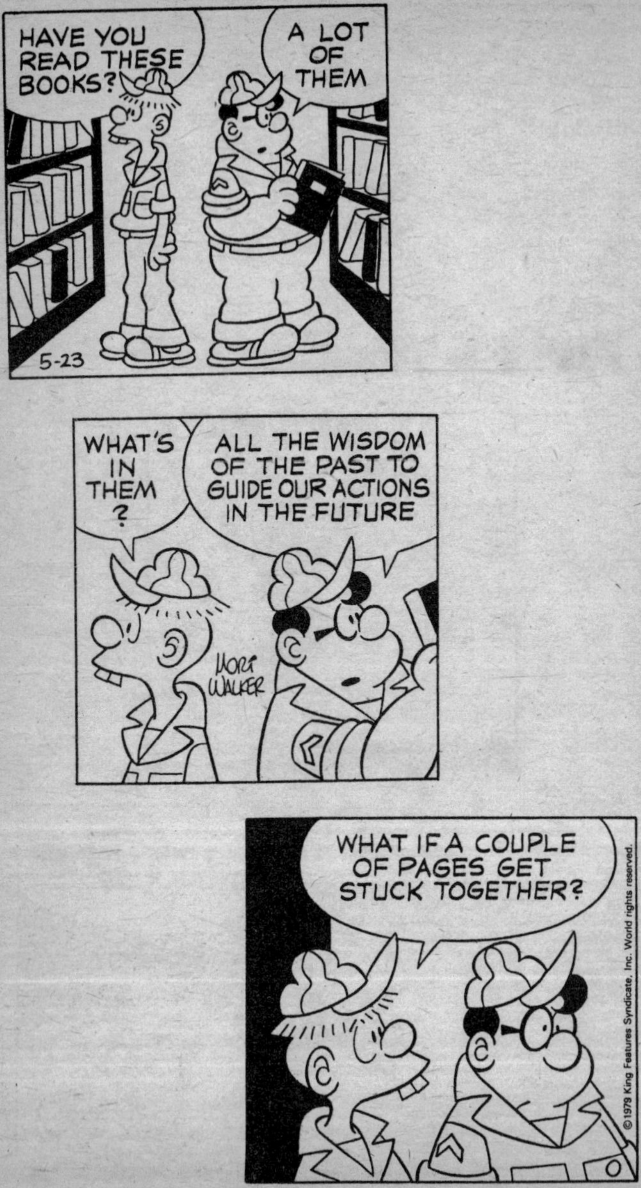
HAVE YOU READ THESE BOOKS?
A LOT OF THEM
5-23
WHAT'S IN THEM ?
ALL THE WISDOM OF THE PAST TO GUIDE OUR ACTIONS IN THE FUTURE
MORT WALKER
WHAT IF A COUPLE OF PAGES GET STUCK TOGETHER?
©1979 King Features Syndicate, Inc. World rights reserved.

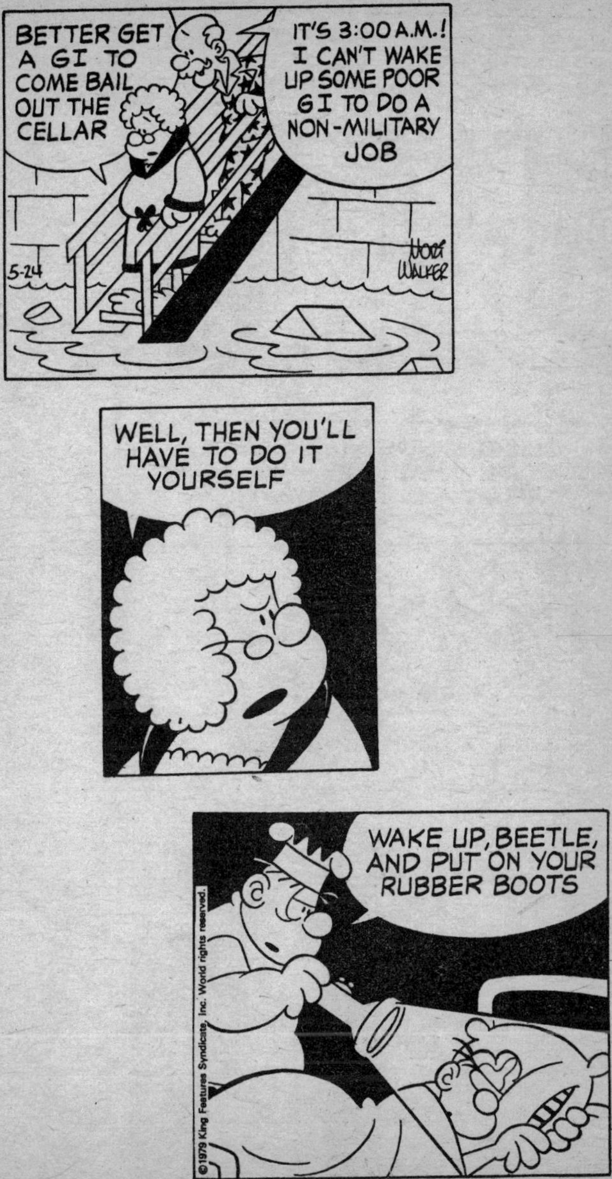
BETTER GET A GI TO COME BAIL OUT THE CELLAR
IT'S 3:00 A.M.! I CAN'T WAKE UP SOME POOR GI TO DO A NON-MILITARY JOB
5-24
MORT WALKER
WELL, THEN YOU'LL HAVE TO DO IT YOURSELF
WAKE UP, BEETLE, AND PUT ON YOUR RUBBER BOOTS
©1979 King Features Syndicate, Inc. World rights reserved.

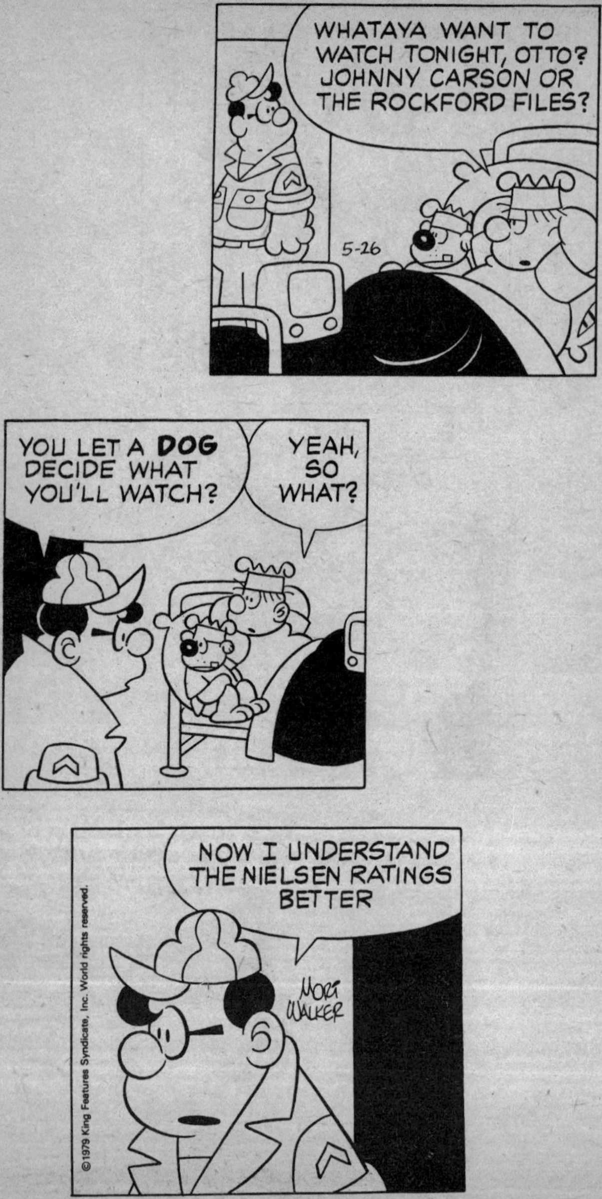
WHATAYA WANT TO WATCH TONIGHT, OTTO? JOHNNY CARSON OR THE ROCKFORD FILES?
5-26
YOU LET A **DOG** DECIDE WHAT YOU'LL WATCH?
YEAH, SO WHAT?
NOW I UNDERSTAND THE NIELSEN RATINGS BETTER
MORT WALKER
©1979 King Features Syndicate, Inc. World rights reserved.

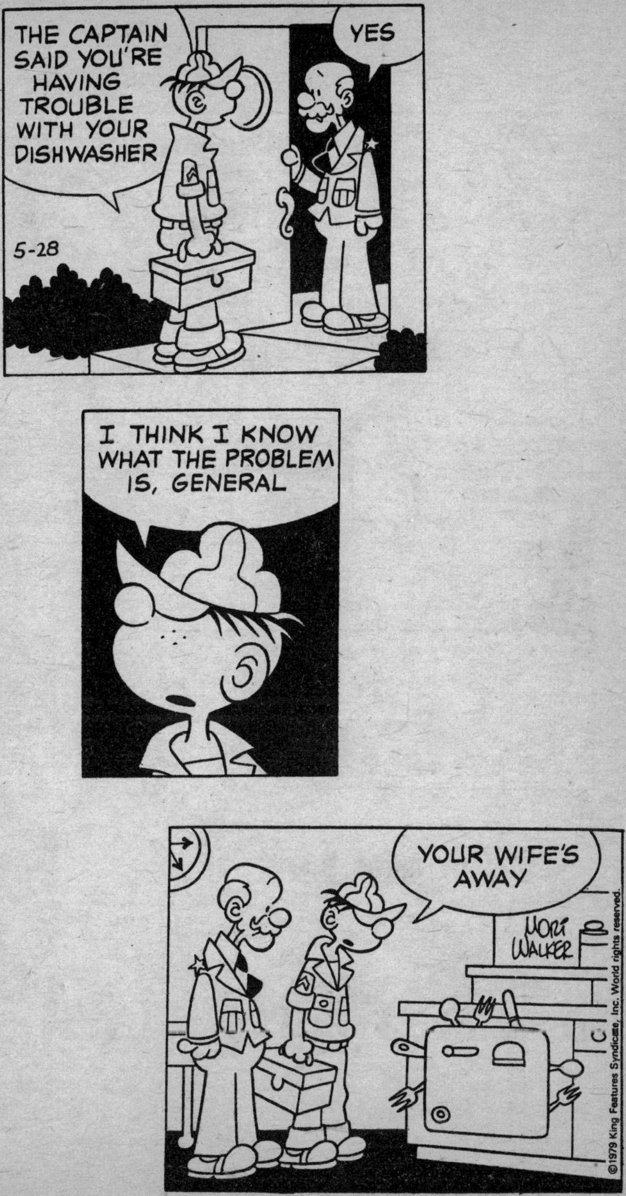
THE CAPTAIN SAID YOU'RE HAVING TROUBLE WITH YOUR DISHWASHER
YES
5-28
I THINK I KNOW WHAT THE PROBLEM IS, GENERAL
YOUR WIFE'S AWAY
MORT WALKER
©1979 King Features Syndicate, Inc. World rights reserved.

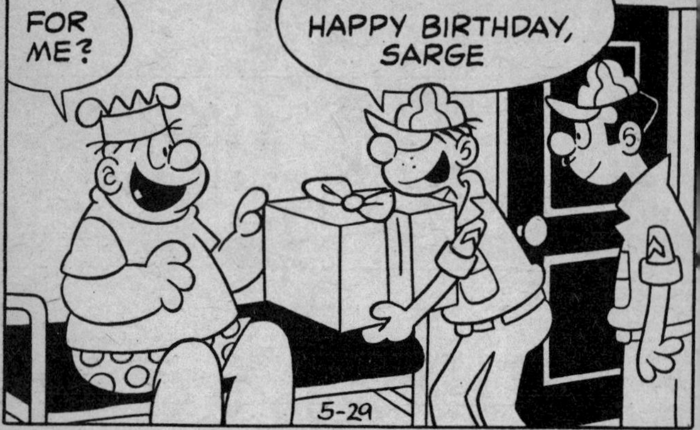
FOR ME?
HAPPY BIRTHDAY, SARGE
5-29

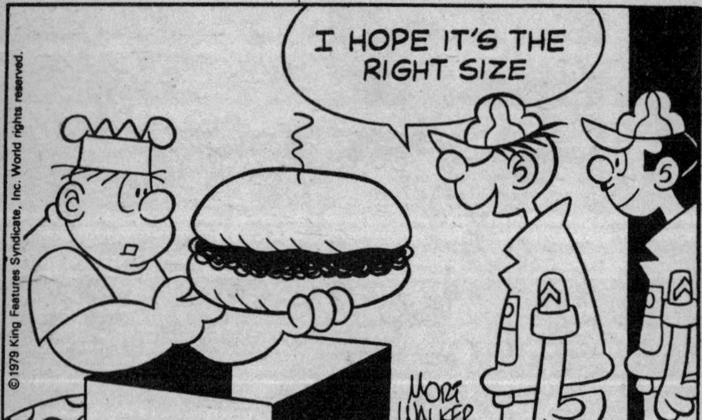
I HOPE IT'S THE RIGHT SIZE
MORT WALKER

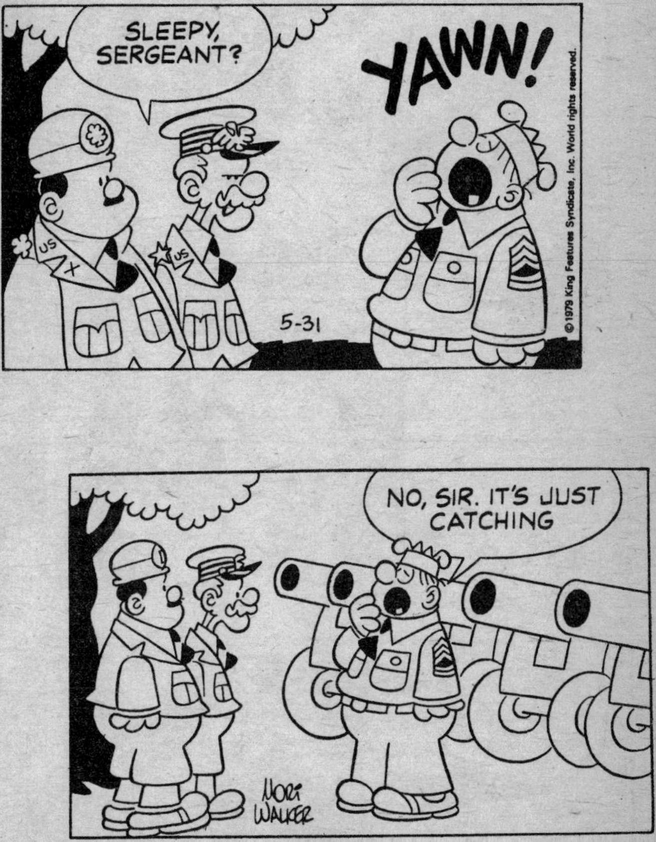
SLEEPY, SERGEANT?
YAWN!
5-31
© 1979 King Features Syndicate, Inc. World rights reserved.
NO, SIR. IT'S JUST CATCHING
MORT WALKER

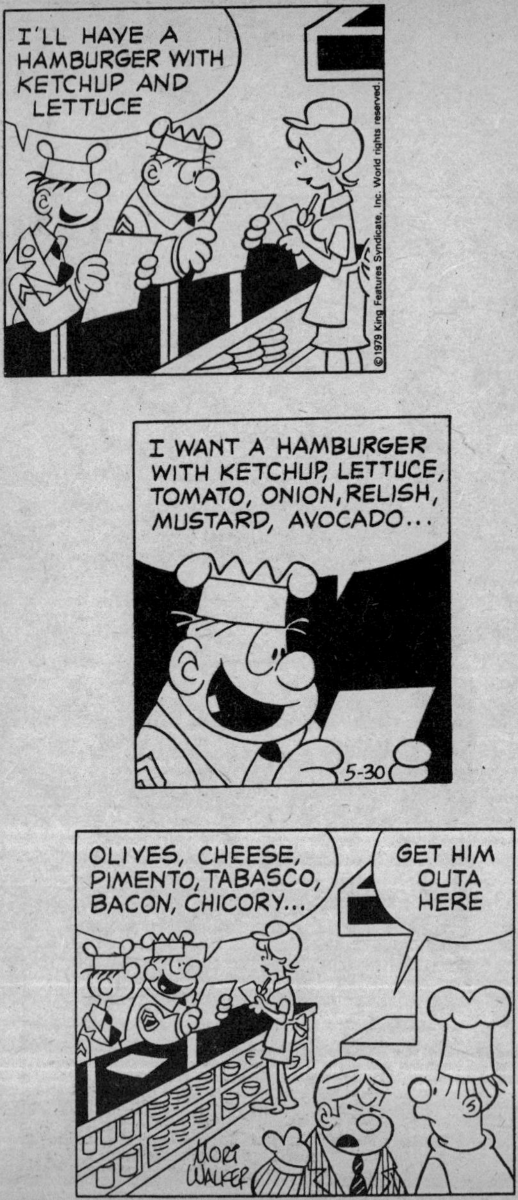
I'LL HAVE A HAMBURGER WITH KETCHUP AND LETTUCE
© 1979 King Features Syndicate, Inc. World rights reserved.
I WANT A HAMBURGER WITH KETCHUP, LETTUCE, TOMATO, ONION, RELISH, MUSTARD, AVOCADO...
5-30
OLIVES, CHEESE, PIMENTO, TABASCO, BACON, CHICORY...
GET HIM OUTA HERE
MORT WALKER

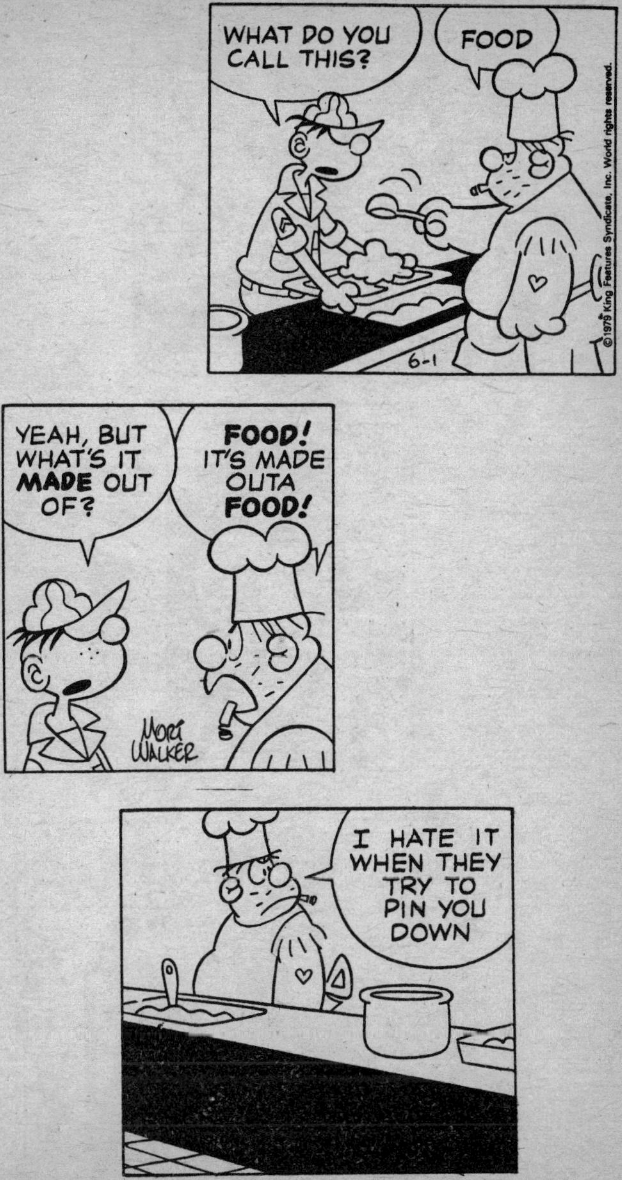
WHAT DO YOU CALL THIS?
FOOD
6-1
YEAH, BUT WHAT'S IT **MADE** OUT OF?
FOOD! IT'S MADE OUTA **FOOD!**
MORT WALKER
I HATE IT WHEN THEY TRY TO PIN YOU DOWN

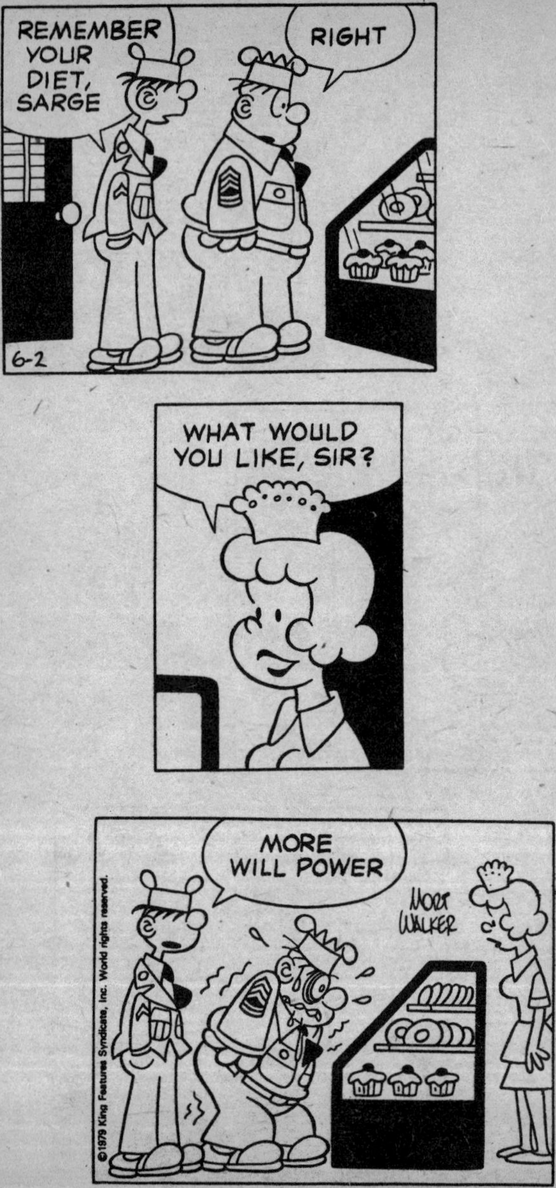
REMEMBER YOUR DIET, SARGE
RIGHT
6-2
WHAT WOULD YOU LIKE, SIR?
MORE WILL POWER
MORT WALKER
©1979 King Features Syndicate, Inc. World rights reserved.

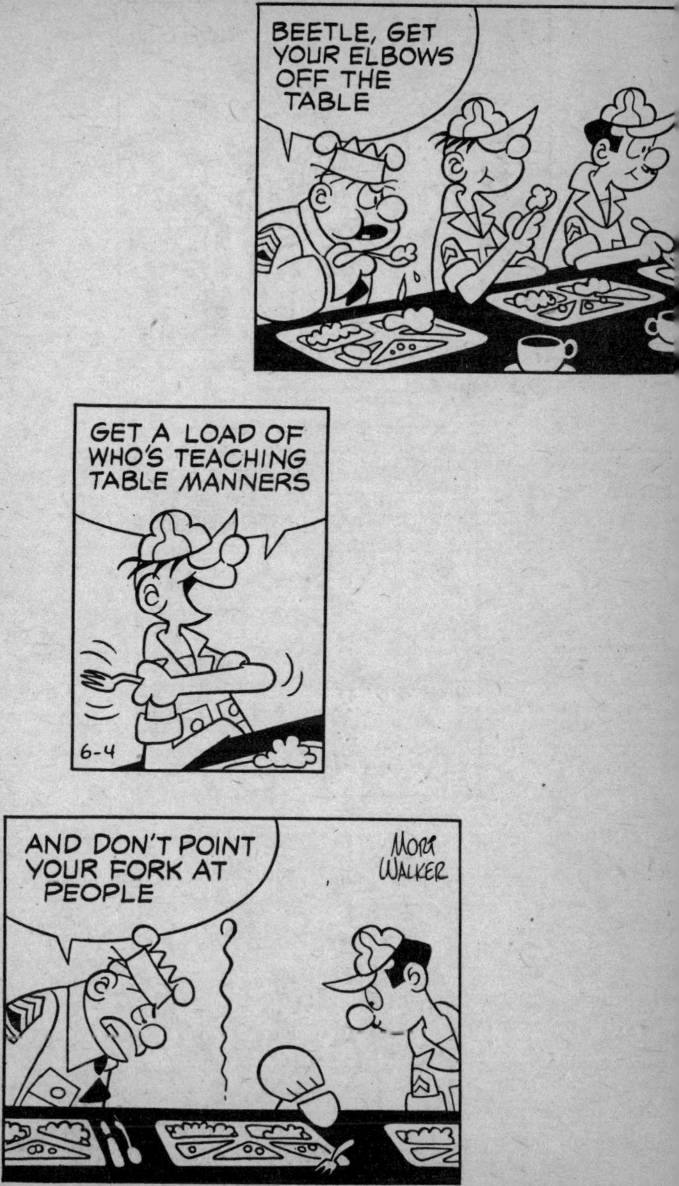
BEETLE, GET YOUR ELBOWS OFF THE TABLE
GET A LOAD OF WHO'S TEACHING TABLE MANNERS
6-4
AND DON'T POINT YOUR FORK AT PEOPLE
MORT WALKER

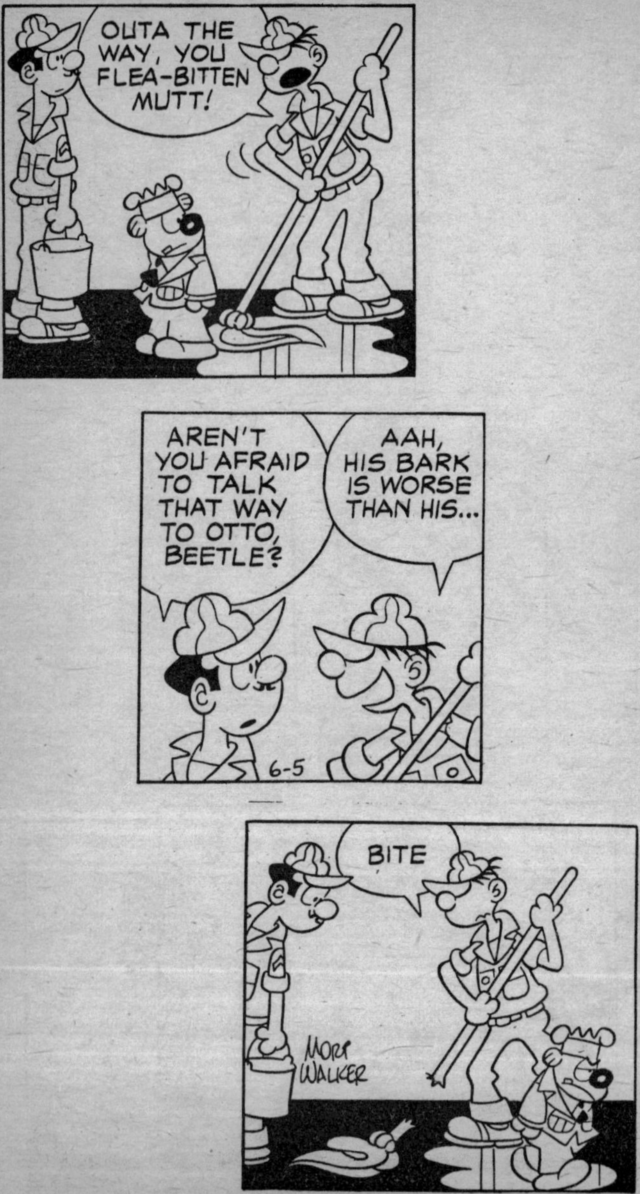
OUTA THE WAY, YOU FLEA-BITTEN MUTT!
AREN'T YOU AFRAID TO TALK THAT WAY TO OTTO, BEETLE?
AAH, HIS BARK IS WORSE THAN HIS...
6-5
BITE
MORT WALKER

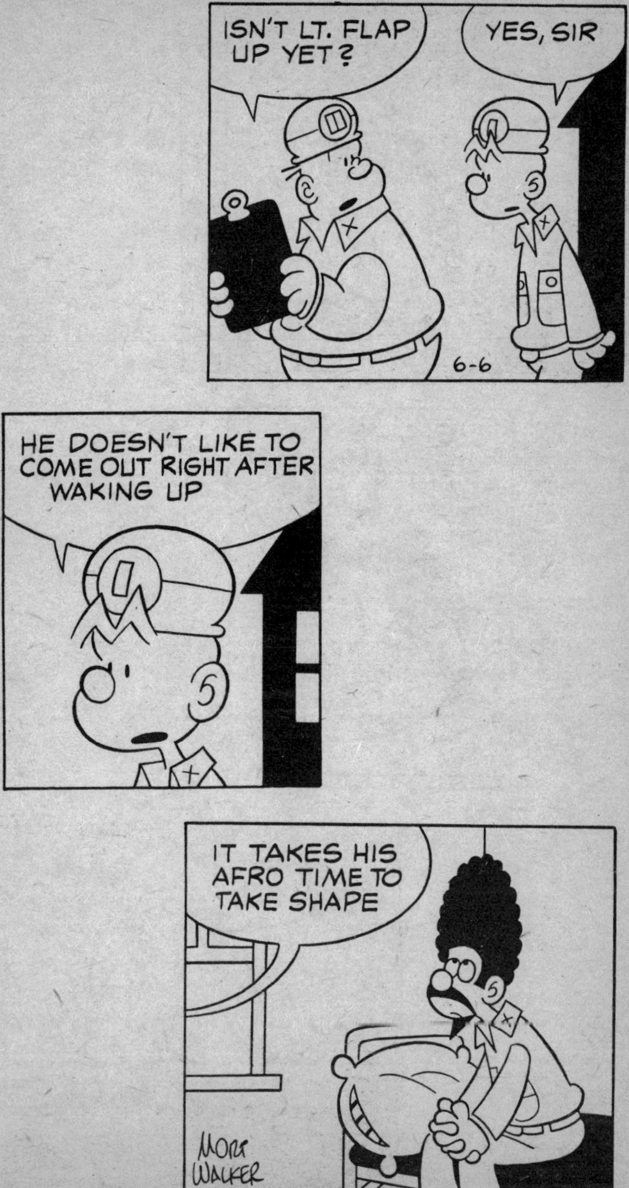
ISN'T LT. FLAP UP YET?
YES, SIR
6-6
HE DOESN'T LIKE TO COME OUT RIGHT AFTER WAKING UP
IT TAKES HIS AFRO TIME TO TAKE SHAPE
MORT WALKER

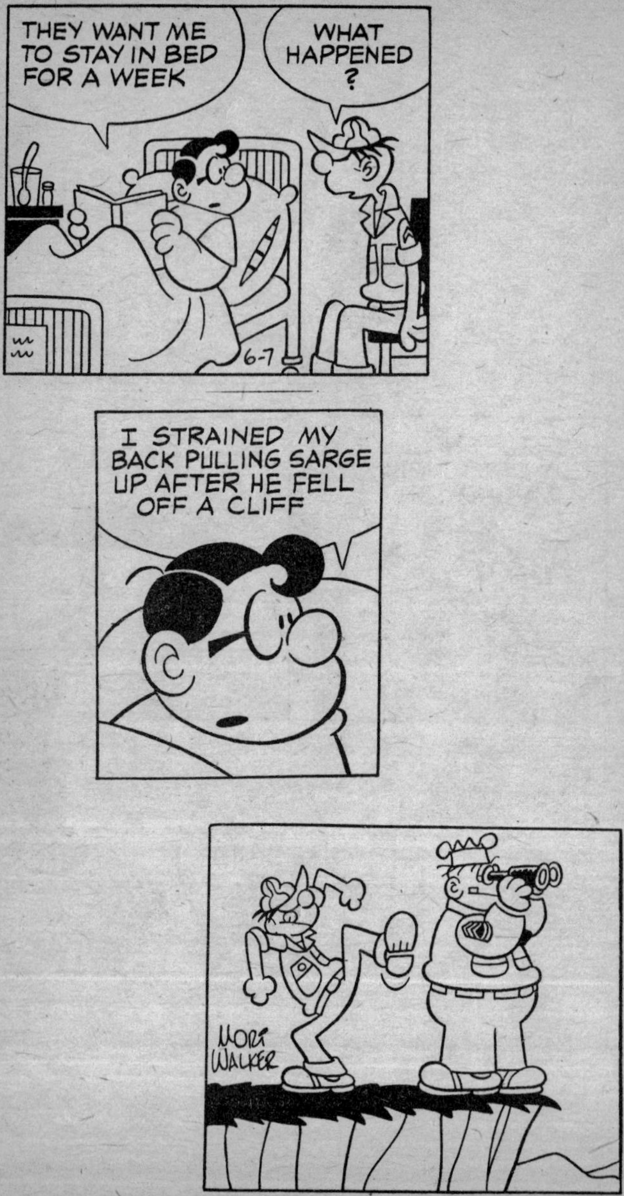
THEY WANT ME TO STAY IN BED FOR A WEEK
WHAT HAPPENED ?
6-7
I STRAINED MY BACK PULLING SARGE UP AFTER HE FELL OFF A CLIFF
MORT WALKER

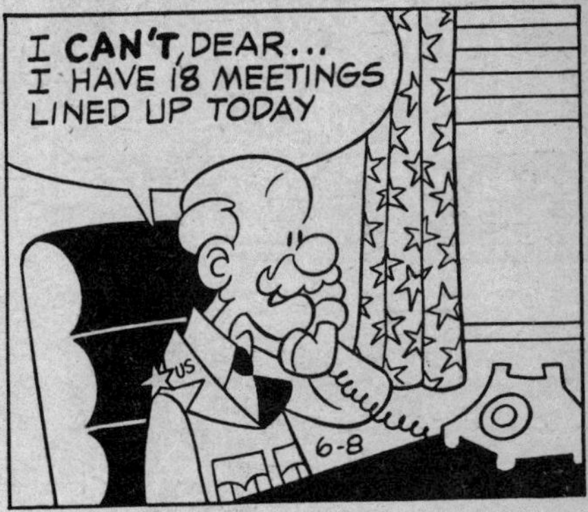
I **CAN'T**, DEAR...
I HAVE 18 MEETINGS
LINED UP TODAY
US
6-8

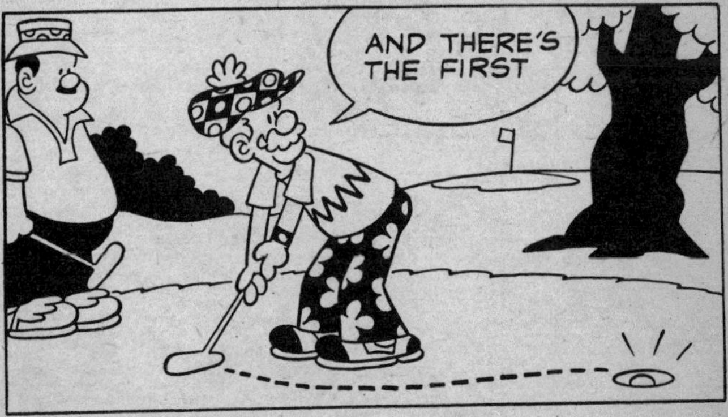
AND THERE'S
THE FIRST

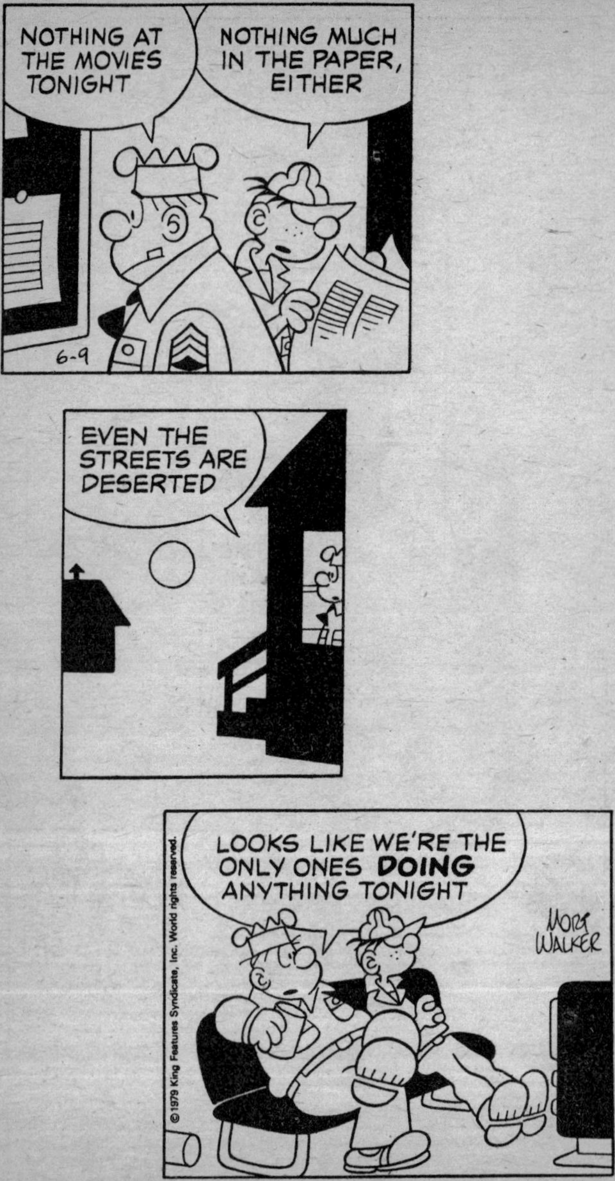
NOTHING AT THE MOVIES TONIGHT
NOTHING MUCH IN THE PAPER, EITHER
6-9
EVEN THE STREETS ARE DESERTED
LOOKS LIKE WE'RE THE ONLY ONES **DOING** ANYTHING TONIGHT
MORT WALKER
© 1979 King Features Syndicate, Inc. World rights reserved.

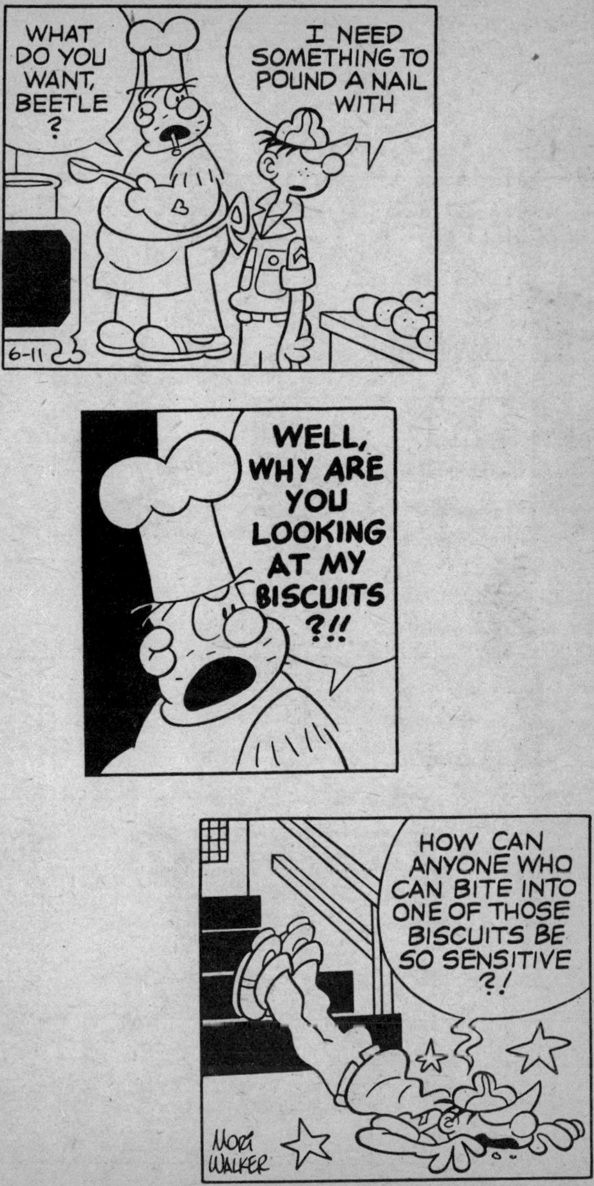
WHAT DO YOU WANT, BEETLE ?
I NEED SOMETHING TO POUND A NAIL WITH
6-11
WELL, WHY ARE YOU LOOKING AT MY BISCUITS ?!!
HOW CAN ANYONE WHO CAN BITE INTO ONE OF THOSE BISCUITS BE SO SENSITIVE ?!
MORT WALKER

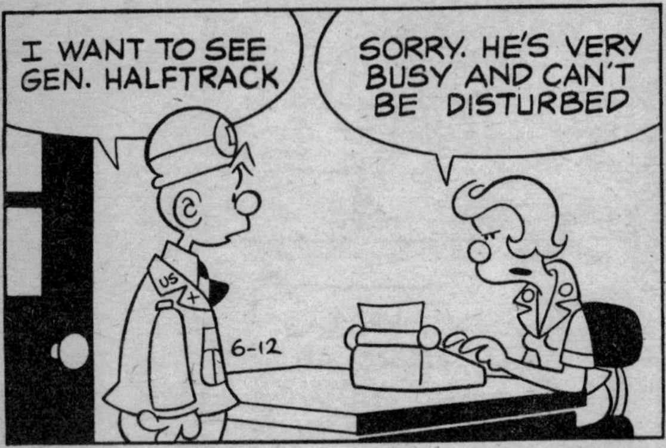
I WANT TO SEE GEN. HALFTRACK
SORRY. HE'S VERY BUSY AND CAN'T BE DISTURBED
6-12

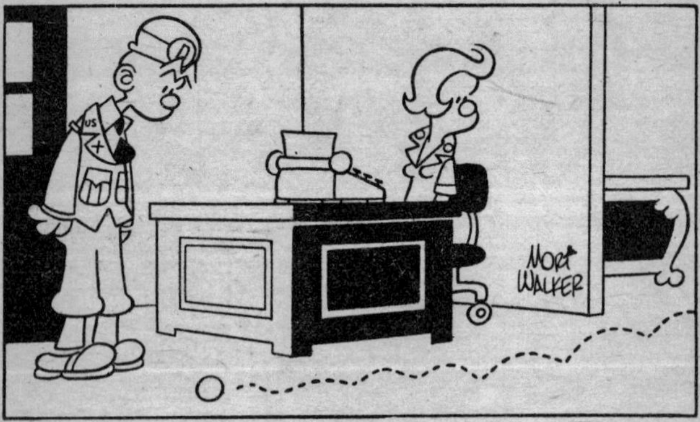
MORT WALKER

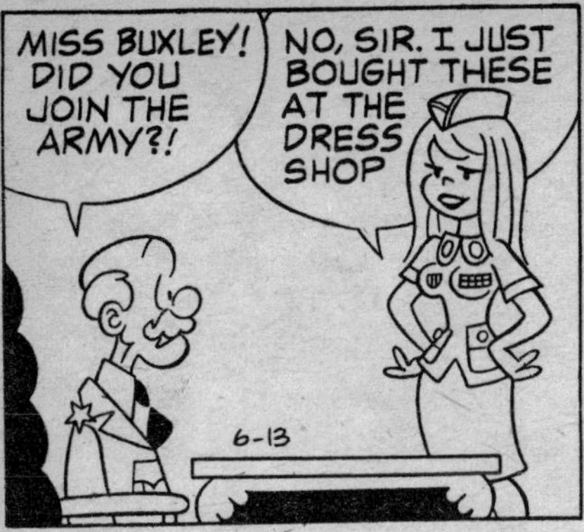
MISS BUXLEY! DID YOU JOIN THE ARMY?!
NO, SIR. I JUST BOUGHT THESE AT THE DRESS SHOP
6-13

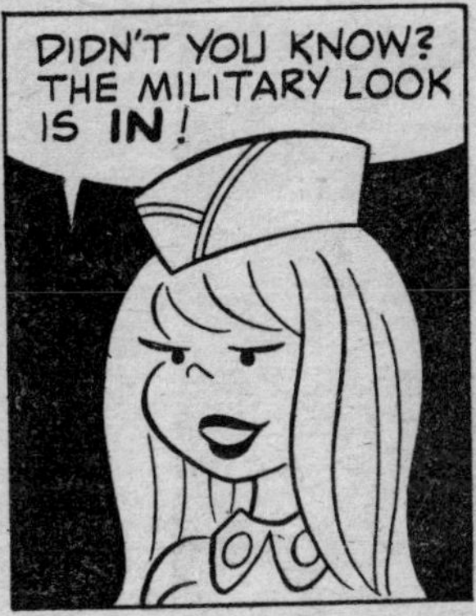
DIDN'T YOU KNOW? THE MILITARY LOOK IS **IN**!

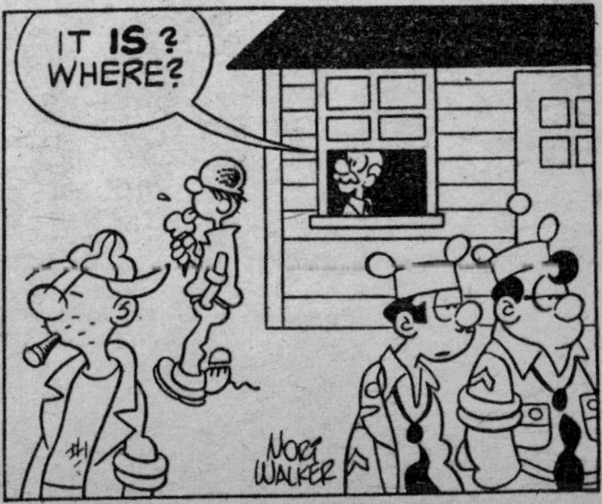
IT **IS**? WHERE?
MORT WALKER

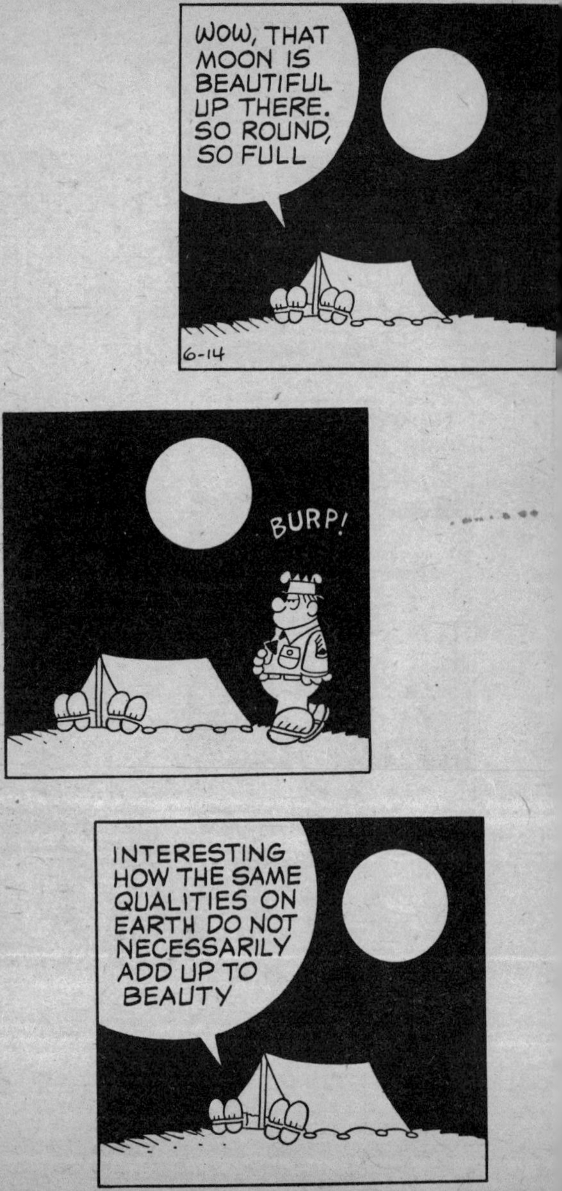
WOW, THAT MOON IS BEAUTIFUL UP THERE. SO ROUND, SO FULL
6-14
BURP!
INTERESTING HOW THE SAME QUALITIES ON EARTH DO NOT NECESSARILY ADD UP TO BEAUTY

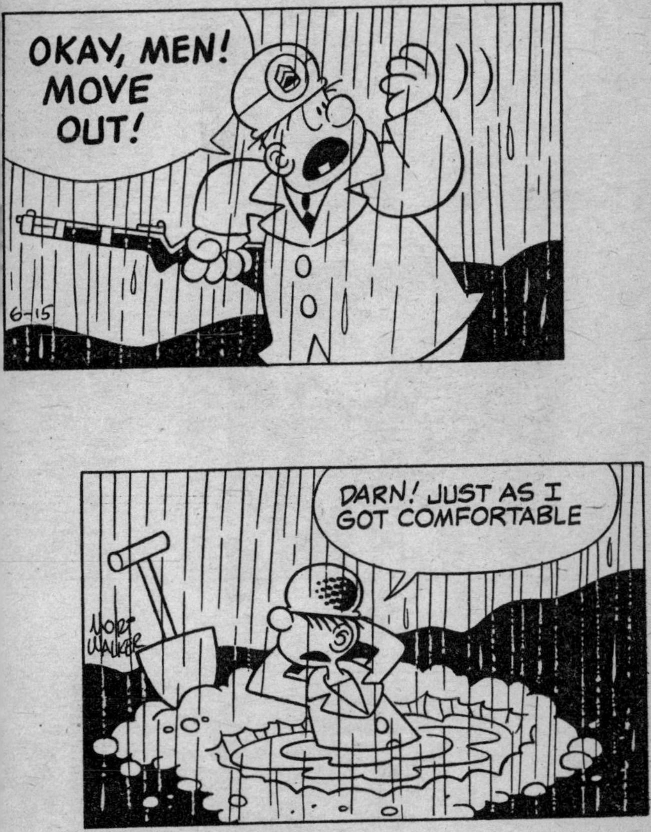
OKAY, MEN! MOVE OUT!
6-15
DARN! JUST AS I GOT COMFORTABLE
MORT WALKER

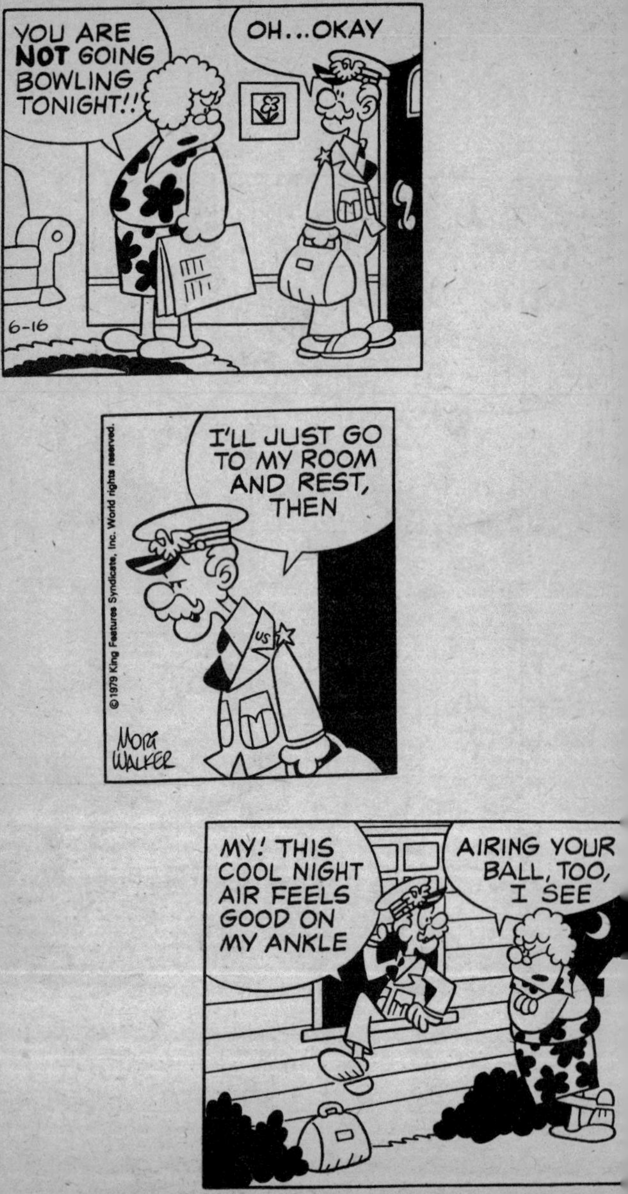
YOU ARE **NOT** GOING BOWLING TONIGHT!!
OH...OKAY
6-16
I'LL JUST GO TO MY ROOM AND REST, THEN
© 1979 King Features Syndicate, Inc. World rights reserved.
MORT WALKER
MY! THIS COOL NIGHT AIR FEELS GOOD ON MY ANKLE
AIRING YOUR BALL, TOO, I SEE

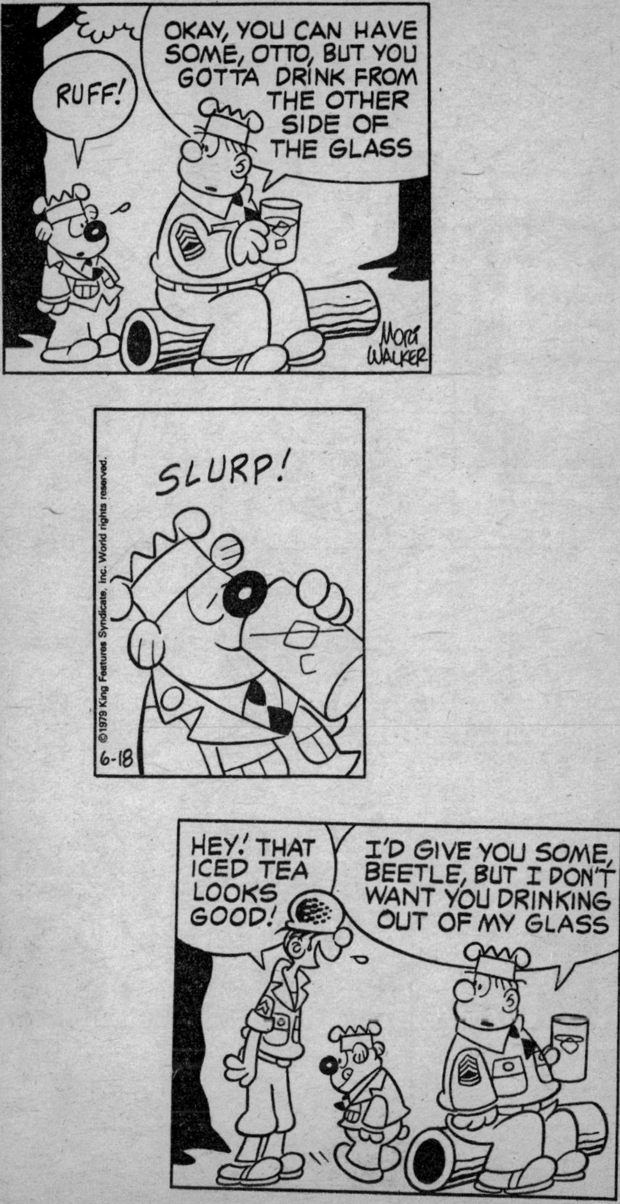
RUFF!
OKAY, YOU CAN HAVE SOME, OTTO, BUT YOU GOTTA DRINK FROM THE OTHER SIDE OF THE GLASS
MORT WALKER
SLURP!
©1979 King Features Syndicate, Inc. World rights reserved.
6-18
HEY! THAT ICED TEA LOOKS GOOD!
I'D GIVE YOU SOME, BEETLE, BUT I DON'T WANT YOU DRINKING OUT OF MY GLASS

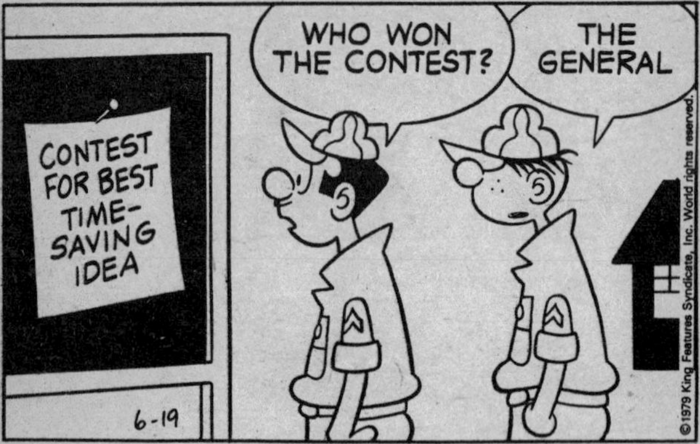
CONTEST FOR BEST TIME-SAVING IDEA
WHO WON THE CONTEST?
THE GENERAL
6-19
©1979 King Features Syndicate, Inc. World rights reserved.

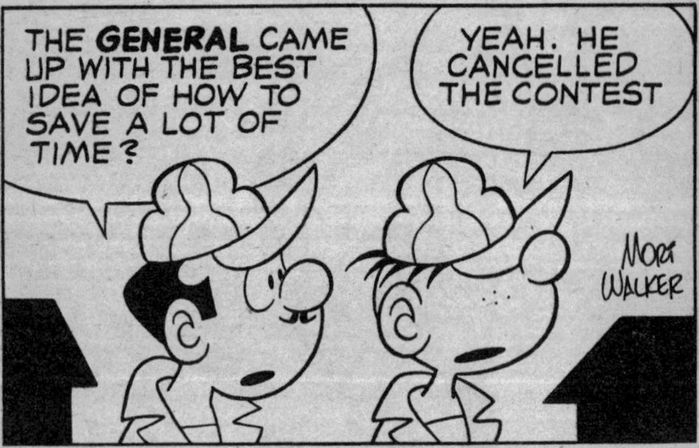
THE **GENERAL** CAME UP WITH THE BEST IDEA OF HOW TO SAVE A LOT OF TIME?
YEAH. HE CANCELLED THE CONTEST
MORT WALKER

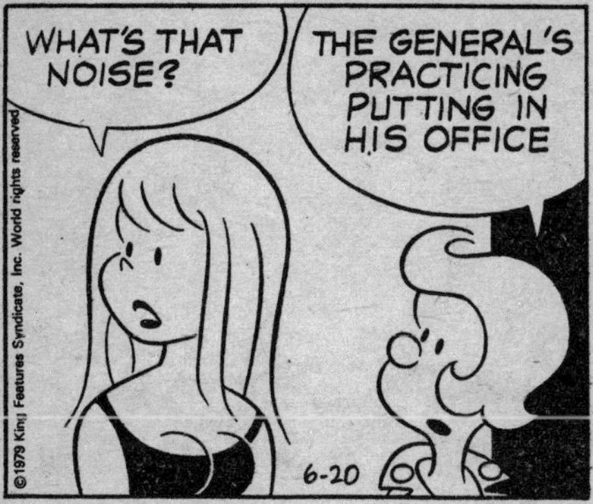
WHAT'S THAT NOISE?
THE GENERAL'S PRACTICING PUTTING IN HIS OFFICE
©1979 King Features Syndicate, Inc. World rights reserved
6-20

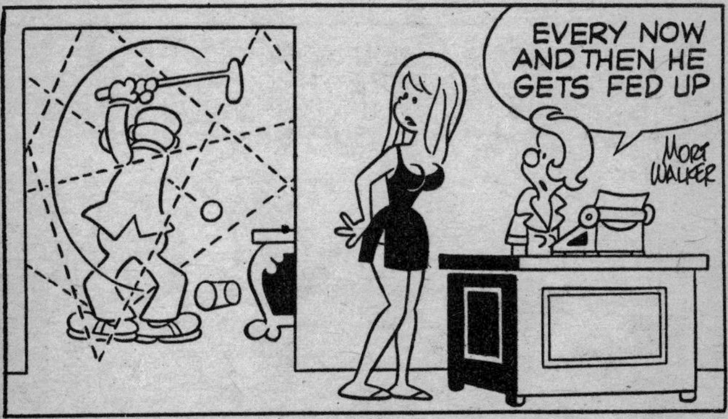
EVERY NOW AND THEN HE GETS FED UP
MORT WALKER

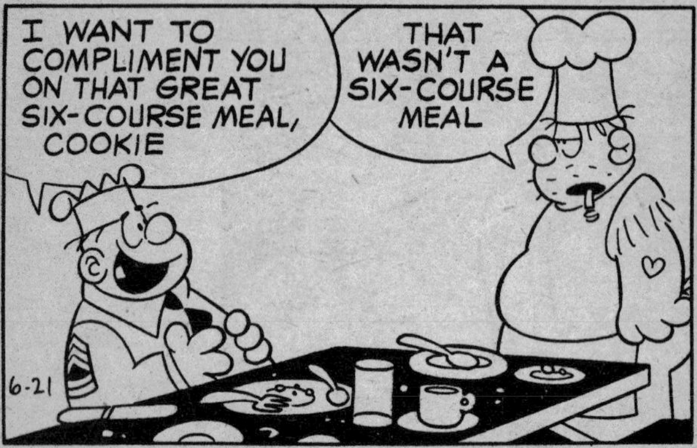
I WANT TO COMPLIMENT YOU ON THAT GREAT SIX-COURSE MEAL, COOKIE
THAT WASN'T A SIX-COURSE MEAL
6-21

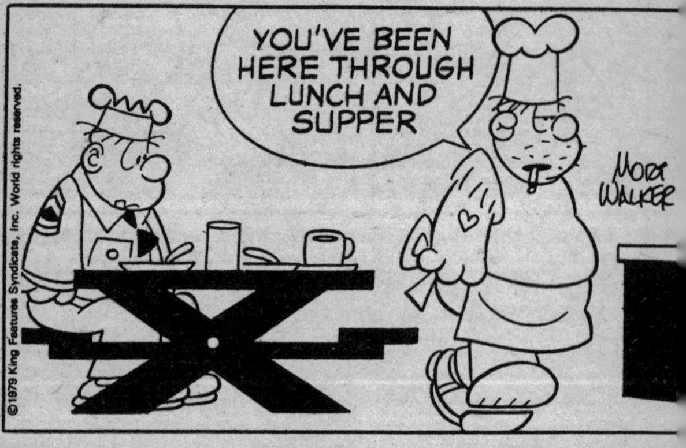
YOU'VE BEEN HERE THROUGH LUNCH AND SUPPER
MORT WALKER
©1979 King Features Syndicate, Inc. World rights reserved.

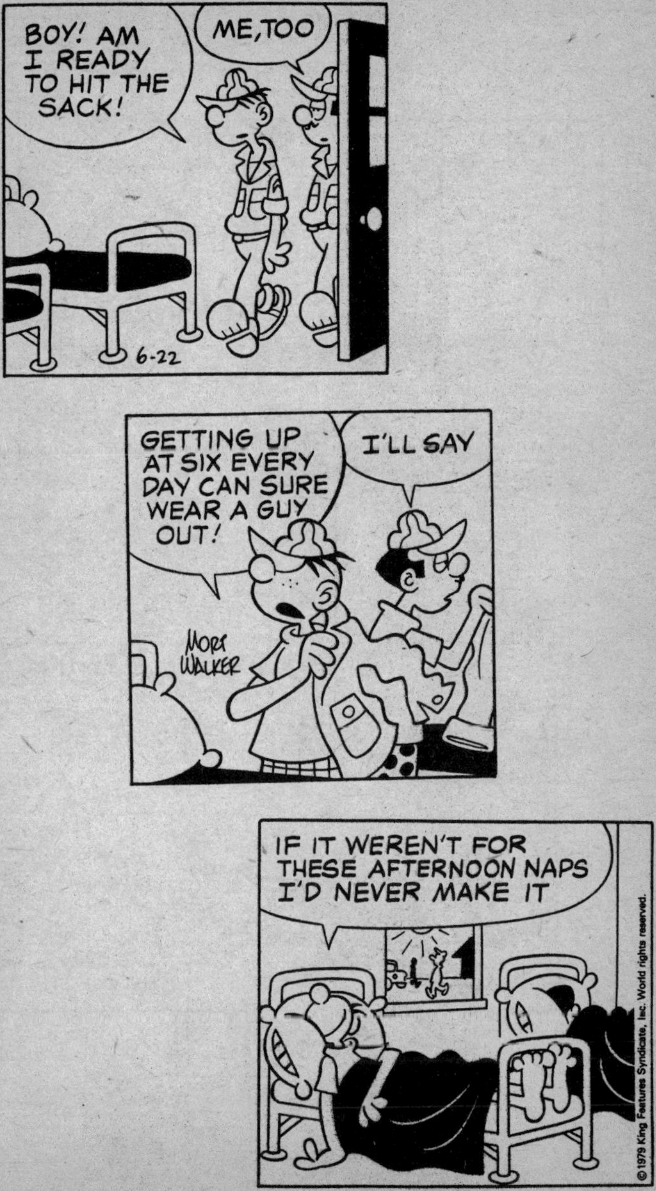
BOY! AM I READY TO HIT THE SACK!
ME, TOO
6-22
GETTING UP AT SIX EVERY DAY CAN SURE WEAR A GUY OUT!
I'LL SAY
MORT WALKER
IF IT WEREN'T FOR THESE AFTERNOON NAPS I'D NEVER MAKE IT
© 1979 King Features Syndicate, Inc. World rights reserved.

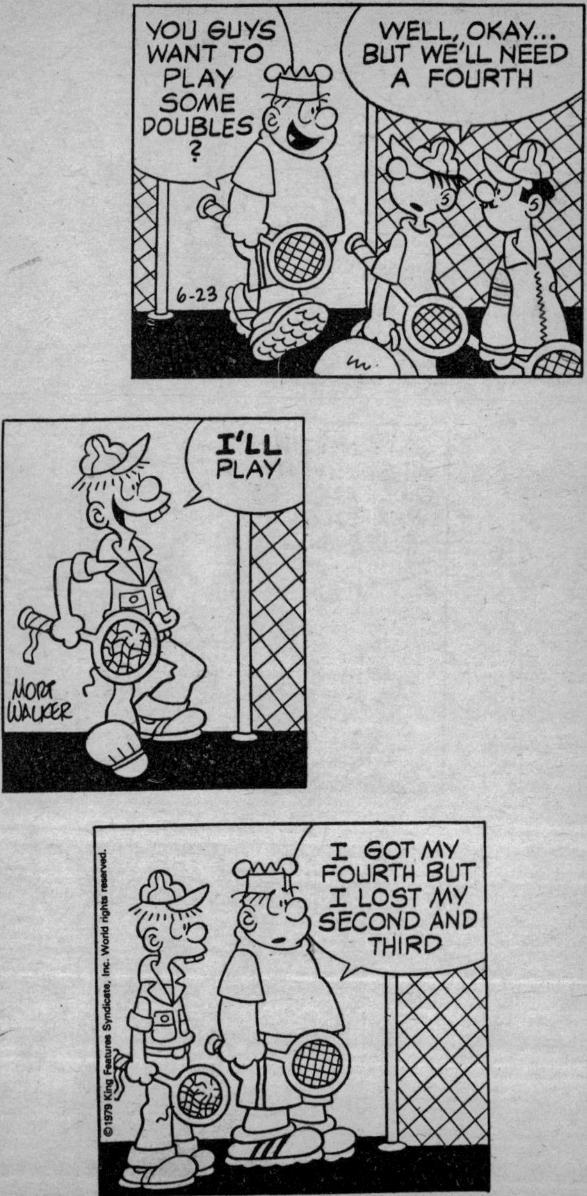
YOU GUYS WANT TO PLAY SOME DOUBLES ?
WELL, OKAY... BUT WE'LL NEED A FOURTH
6-23
I'LL PLAY
MORT WALKER
I GOT MY FOURTH BUT I LOST MY SECOND AND THIRD
©1979 King Features Syndicate, Inc. World rights reserved.

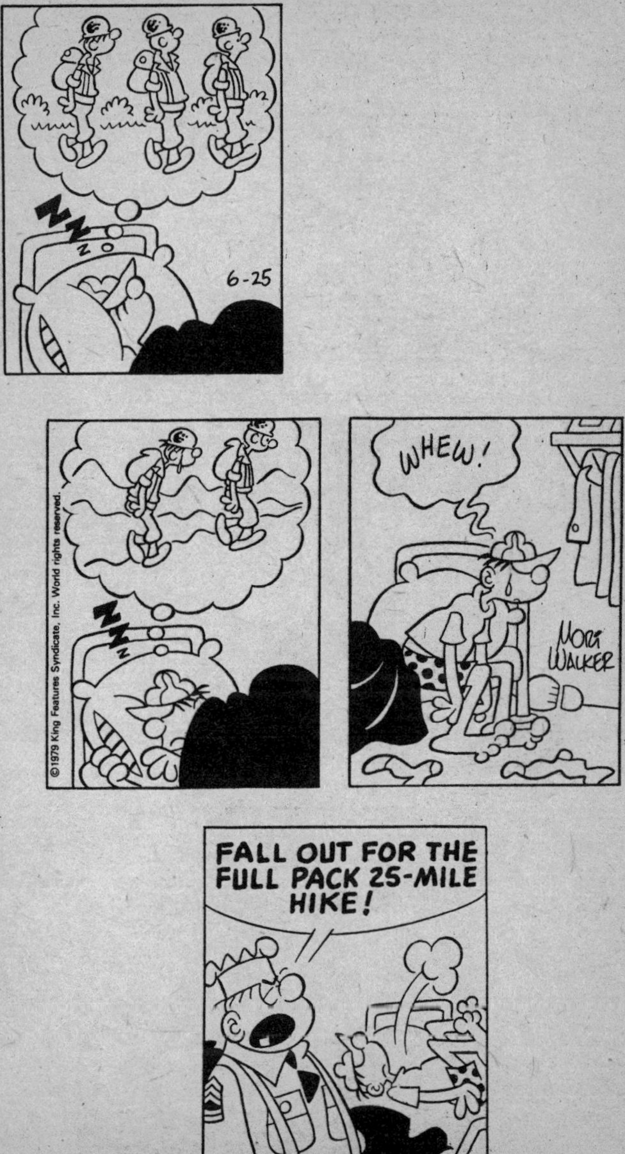
Z Z z o
6-25
Z Z z
©1979 King Features Syndicate, Inc. World rights reserved.
WHEW!
MORT WALKER
FALL OUT FOR THE FULL PACK 25-MILE HIKE!

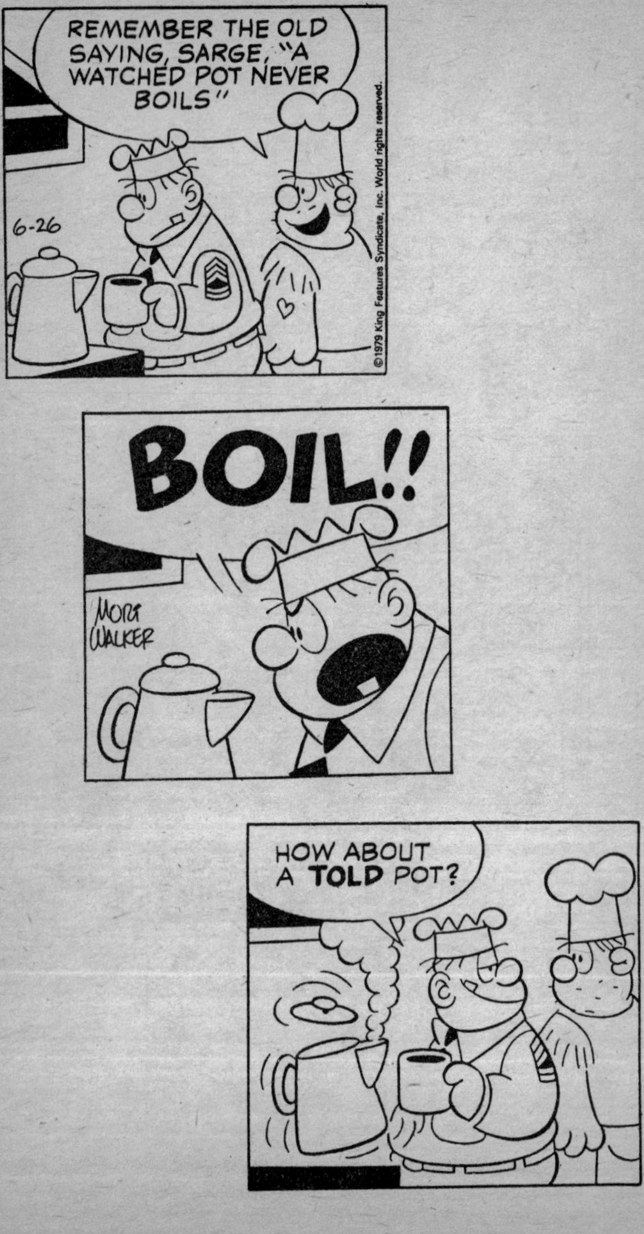
REMEMBER THE OLD SAYING, SARGE, "A WATCHED POT NEVER BOILS"
6-26
©1979 King Features Syndicate, Inc. World rights reserved.
BOIL!!
MORT WALKER
HOW ABOUT A **TOLD** POT?

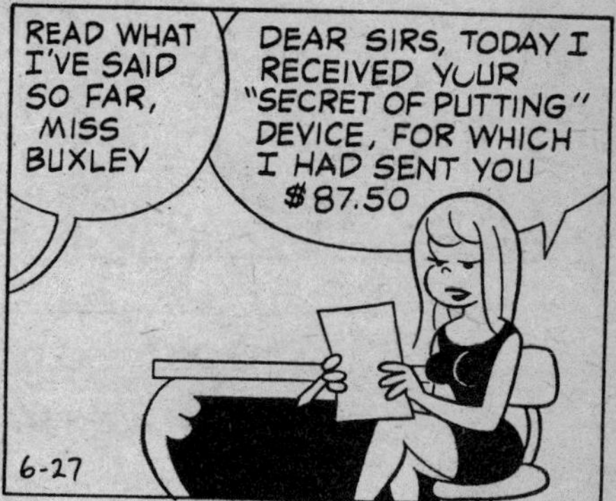
READ WHAT I'VE SAID SO FAR, MISS BUXLEY
DEAR SIRS, TODAY I RECEIVED YOUR "SECRET OF PUTTING" DEVICE, FOR WHICH I HAD SENT YOU $87.50
6-27

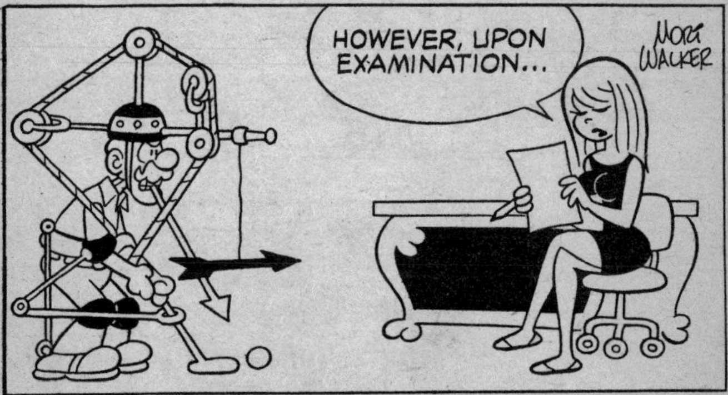
HOWEVER, UPON EXAMINATION...
MORT WALKER

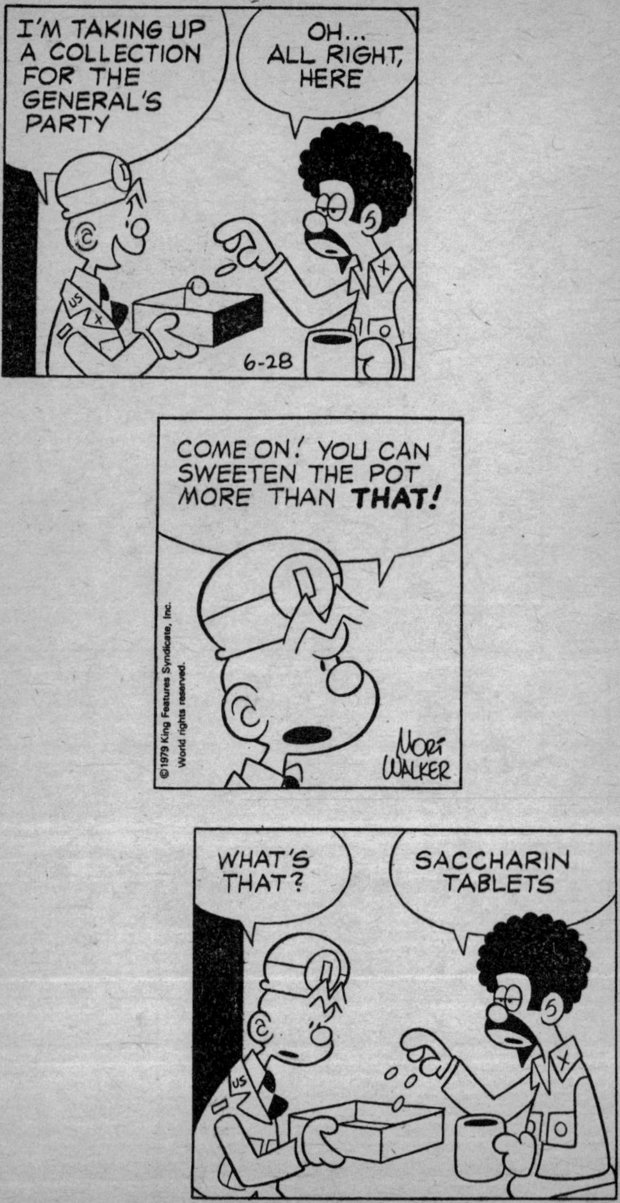
I'M TAKING UP A COLLECTION FOR THE GENERAL'S PARTY
OH... ALL RIGHT, HERE
6-28
COME ON! YOU CAN SWEETEN THE POT MORE THAN **THAT!**
©1979 King Features Syndicate, Inc. World rights reserved.
MORT WALKER
WHAT'S THAT?
SACCHARIN TABLETS

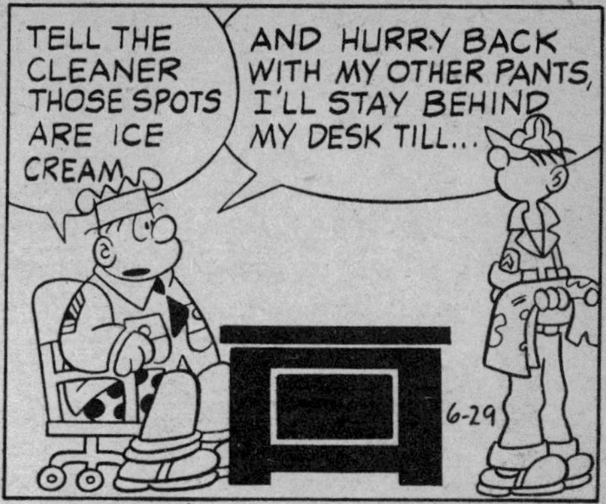
TELL THE CLEANER THOSE SPOTS ARE ICE CREAM
AND HURRY BACK WITH MY OTHER PANTS, I'LL STAY BEHIND MY DESK TILL...
6-29

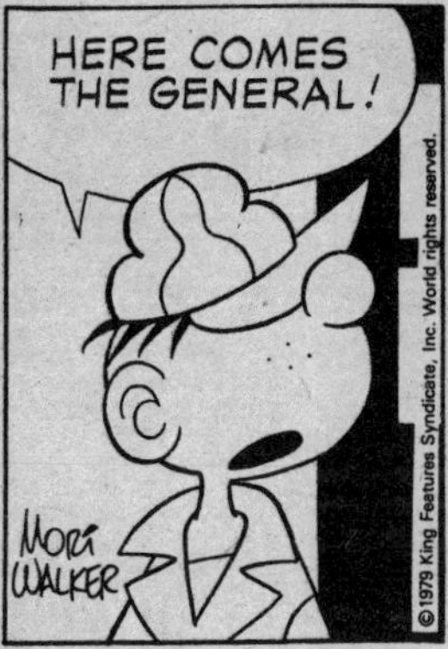
HERE COMES THE GENERAL!
MORT WALKER
© 1979 King Features Syndicate, Inc. World rights reserved.

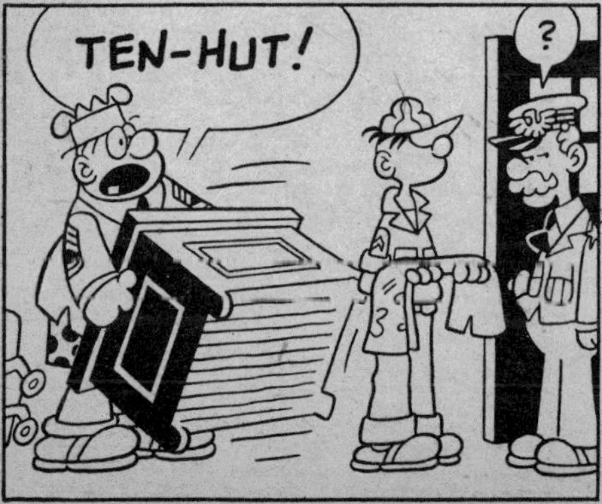
TEN-HUT!
?

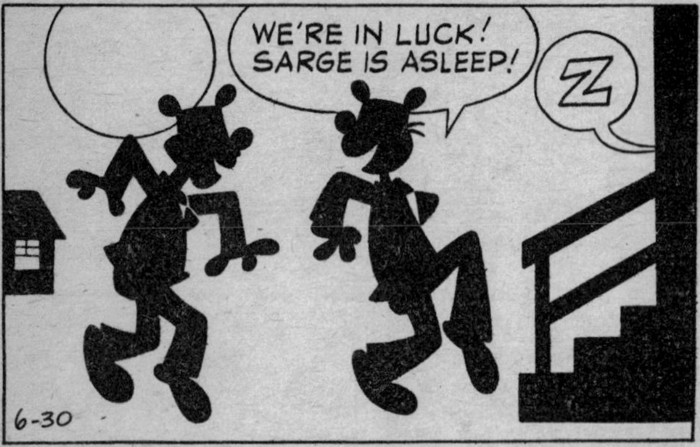
WE'RE IN LUCK! SARGE IS ASLEEP!
Z
6-30

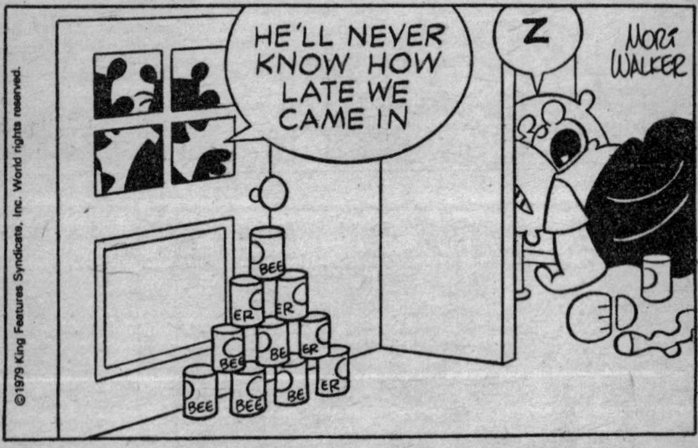
HE'LL NEVER KNOW HOW LATE WE CAME IN
Z
MORT WALKER

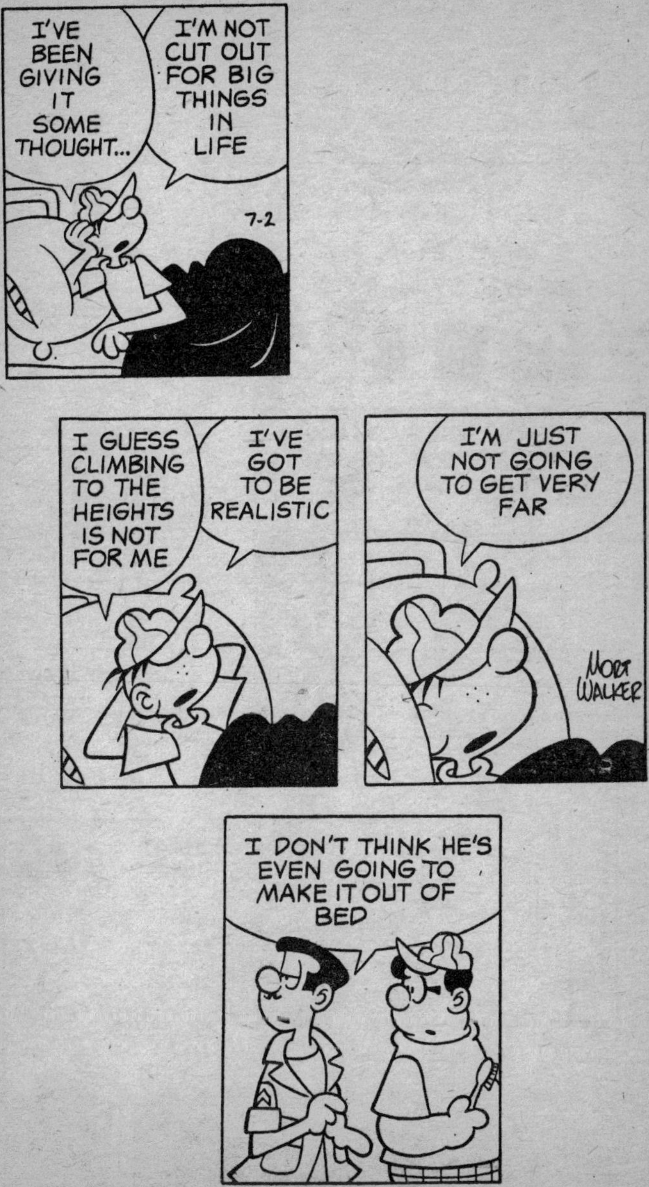

I'VE BEEN GIVING IT SOME THOUGHT...
I'M NOT CUT OUT FOR BIG THINGS IN LIFE
7-2
I GUESS CLIMBING TO THE HEIGHTS IS NOT FOR ME
I'VE GOT TO BE REALISTIC
I'M JUST NOT GOING TO GET VERY FAR
MORT WALKER
I DON'T THINK HE'S EVEN GOING TO MAKE IT OUT OF BED

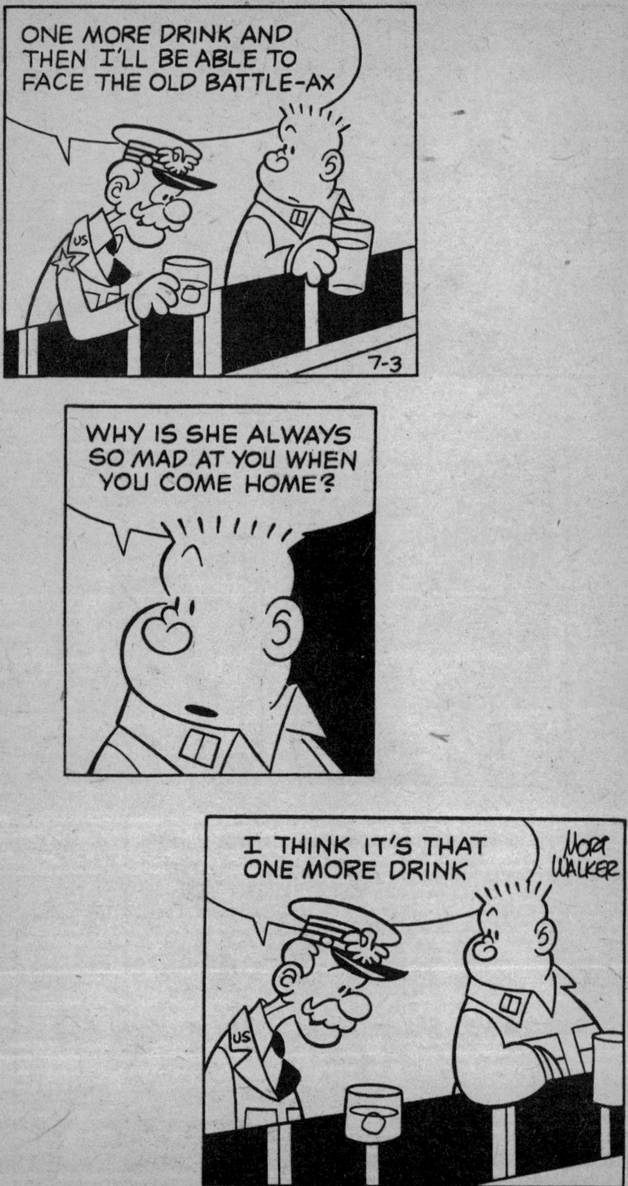
ONE MORE DRINK AND THEN I'LL BE ABLE TO FACE THE OLD BATTLE-AX
US
7-3
WHY IS SHE ALWAYS SO MAD AT YOU WHEN YOU COME HOME?
I THINK IT'S THAT ONE MORE DRINK
US
MORT WALKER

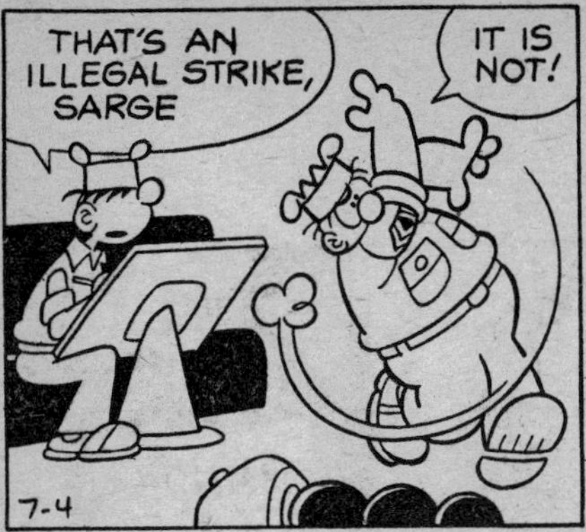
THAT'S AN ILLEGAL STRIKE, SARGE
IT IS NOT!
7-4

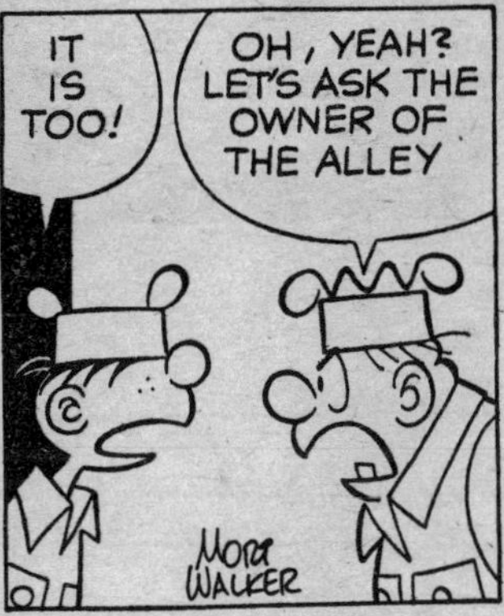
IT IS TOO!
OH, YEAH? LET'S ASK THE OWNER OF THE ALLEY
MORT WALKER

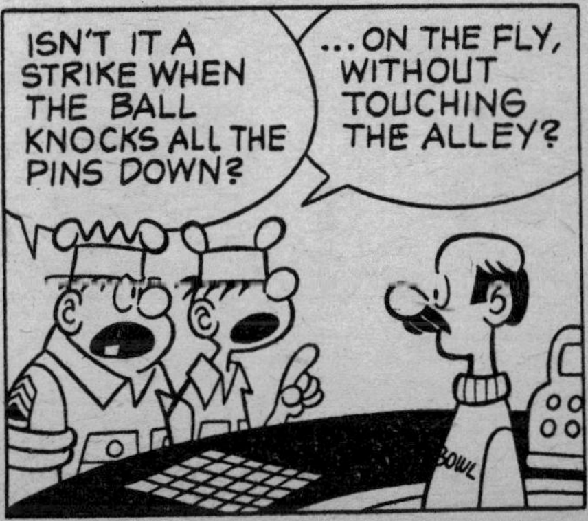
ISN'T IT A STRIKE WHEN THE BALL KNOCKS ALL THE PINS DOWN?
...ON THE FLY, WITHOUT TOUCHING THE ALLEY?
BOWL

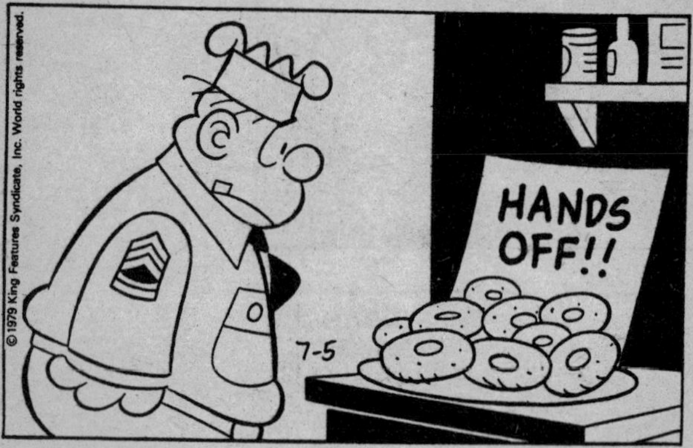
©1979 King Features Syndicate, Inc. World rights reserved.
HANDS OFF!!
7-5

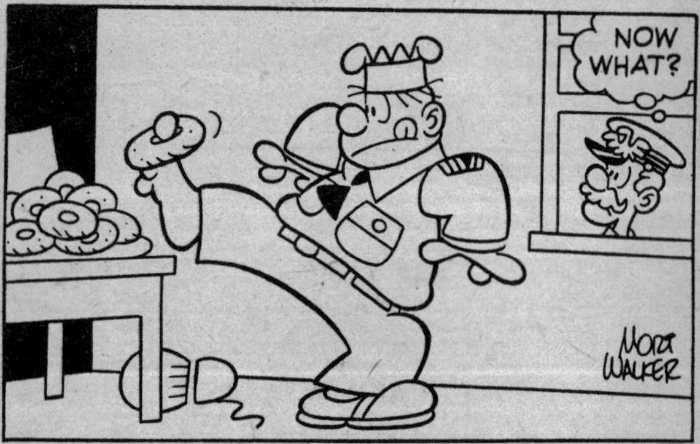
NOW WHAT?
MORT WALKER

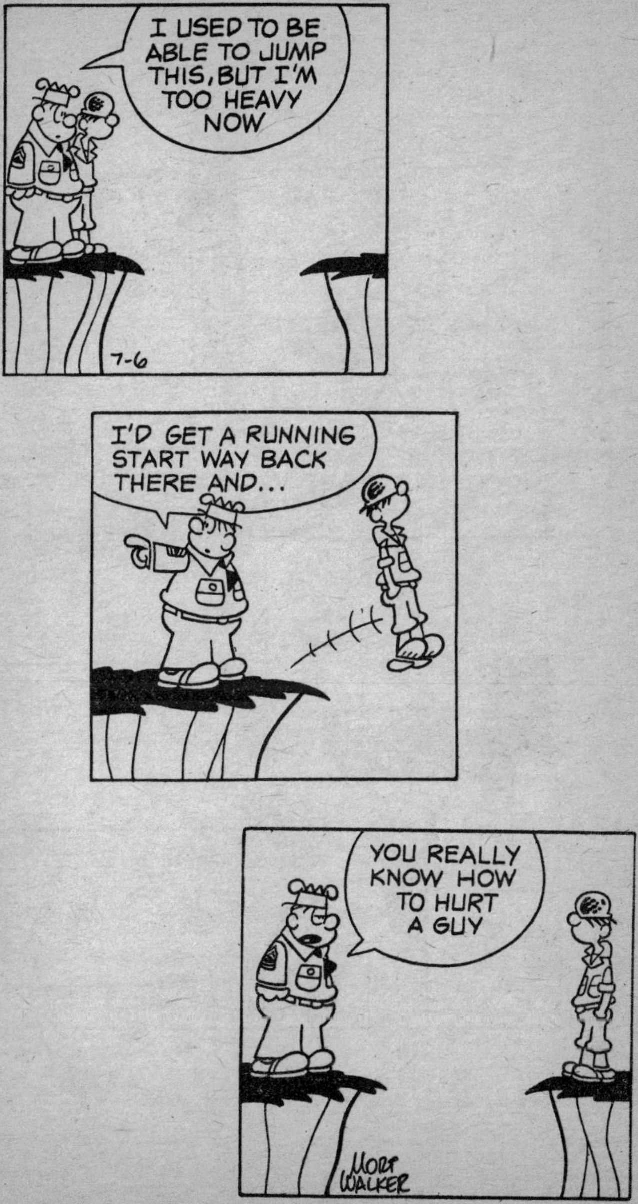

I USED TO BE ABLE TO JUMP THIS, BUT I'M TOO HEAVY NOW
7-6
I'D GET A RUNNING START WAY BACK THERE AND...
YOU REALLY KNOW HOW TO HURT A GUY
MORT WALKER

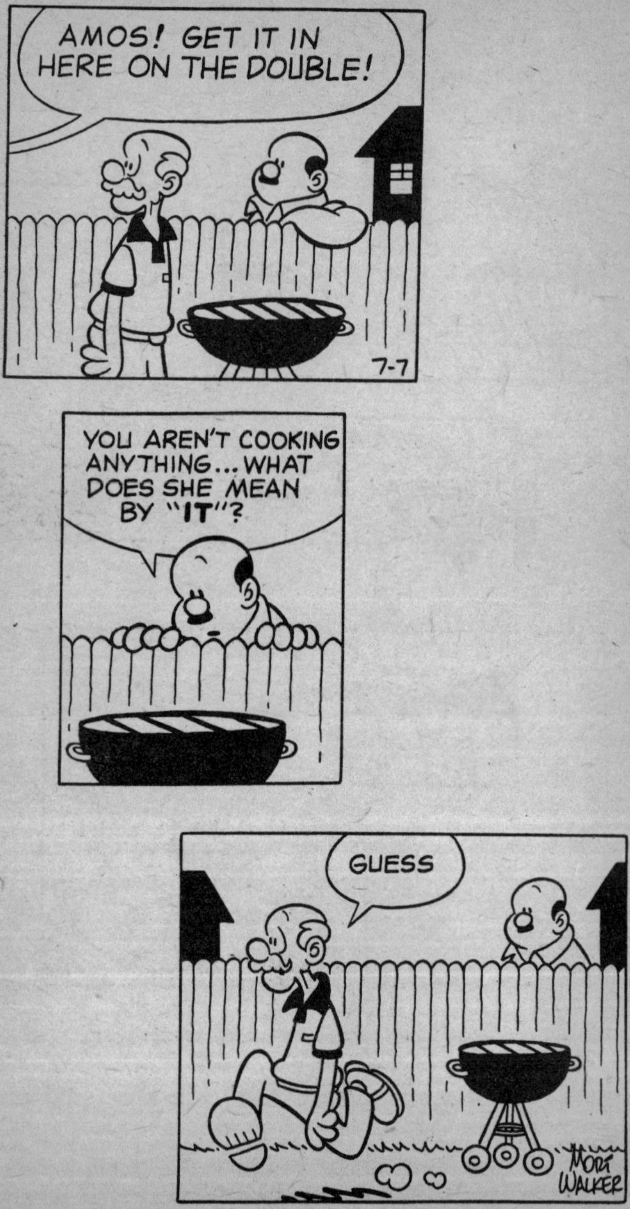
AMOS! GET IT IN HERE ON THE DOUBLE!
7-7
YOU AREN'T COOKING ANYTHING... WHAT DOES SHE MEAN BY "IT"?
GUESS
MORT WALKER

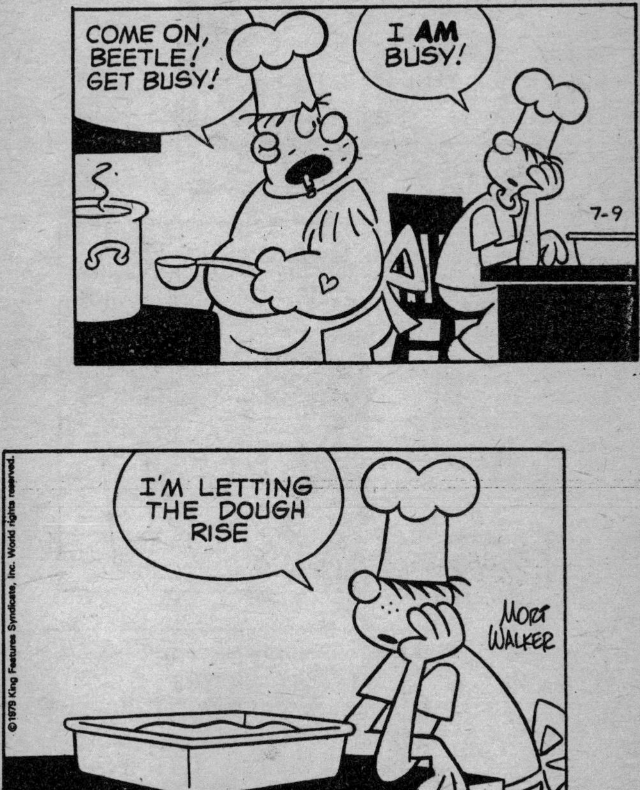
COME ON, BEETLE! GET BUSY!
I AM BUSY!
7-9
I'M LETTING THE DOUGH RISE
MORT WALKER

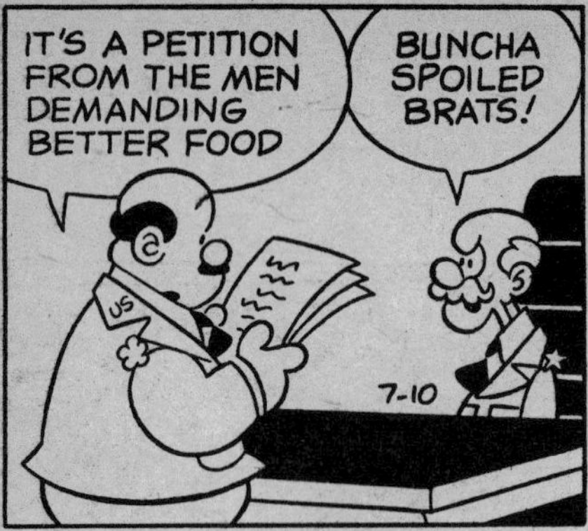
IT'S A PETITION FROM THE MEN DEMANDING BETTER FOOD
BUNCHA SPOILED BRATS!
7-10

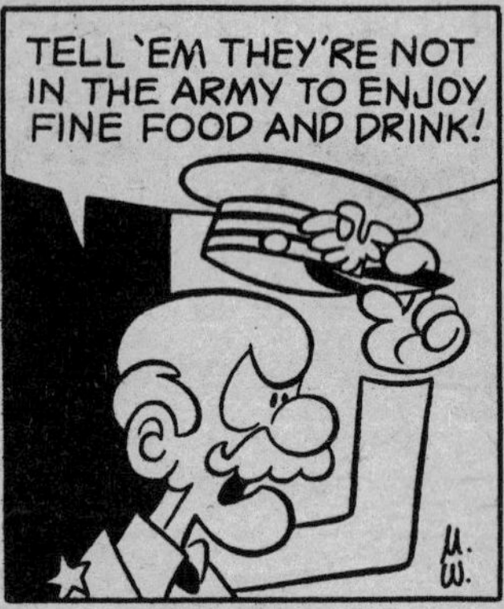
TELL 'EM THEY'RE NOT IN THE ARMY TO ENJOY FINE FOOD AND DRINK!

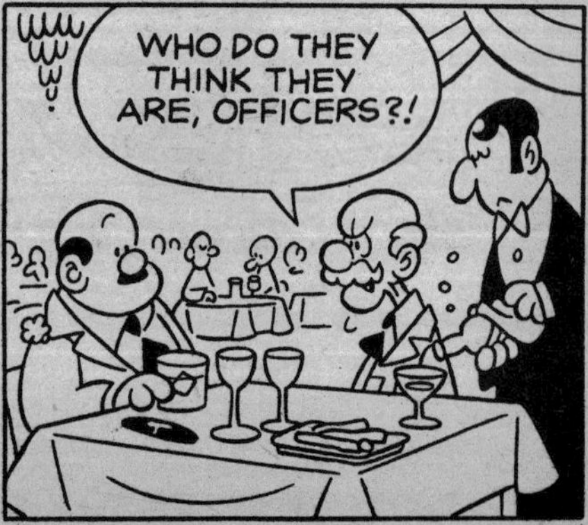
WHO DO THEY THINK THEY ARE, OFFICERS?!

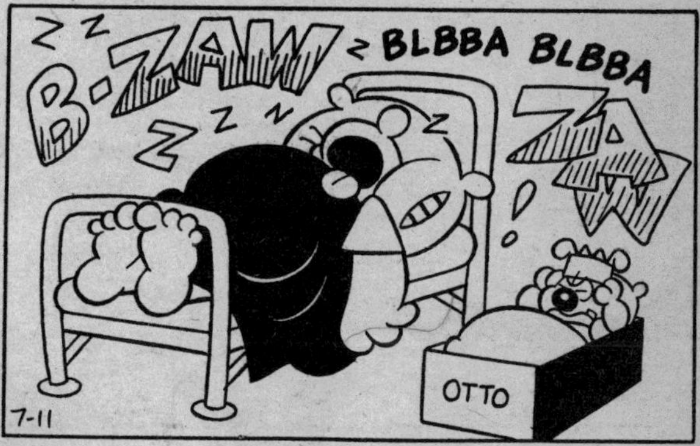
Z Z
B-ZAW
Z BLBBA BLBBA
Z Z Z Z
Z
ZAW
OTTO
7-11

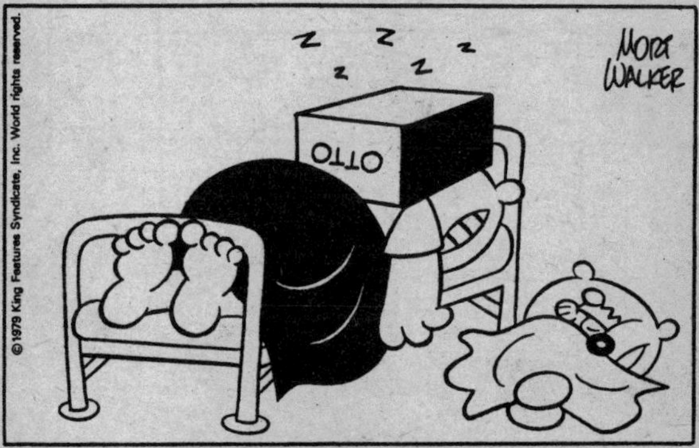
Z Z Z Z Z Z
MORT WALKER
OTTO
© 1979 King Features Syndicate, Inc. World rights reserved.

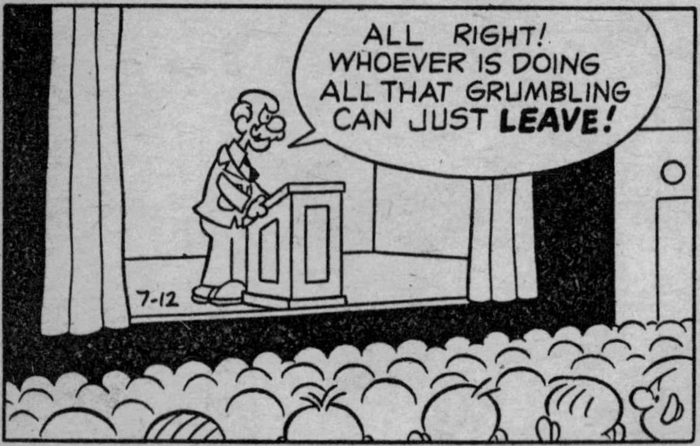
ALL RIGHT! WHOEVER IS DOING ALL THAT GRUMBLING CAN JUST **LEAVE!**
7-12

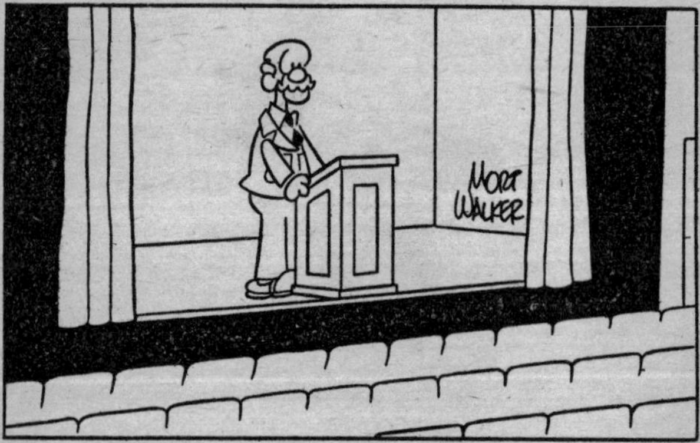
MORT WALKER

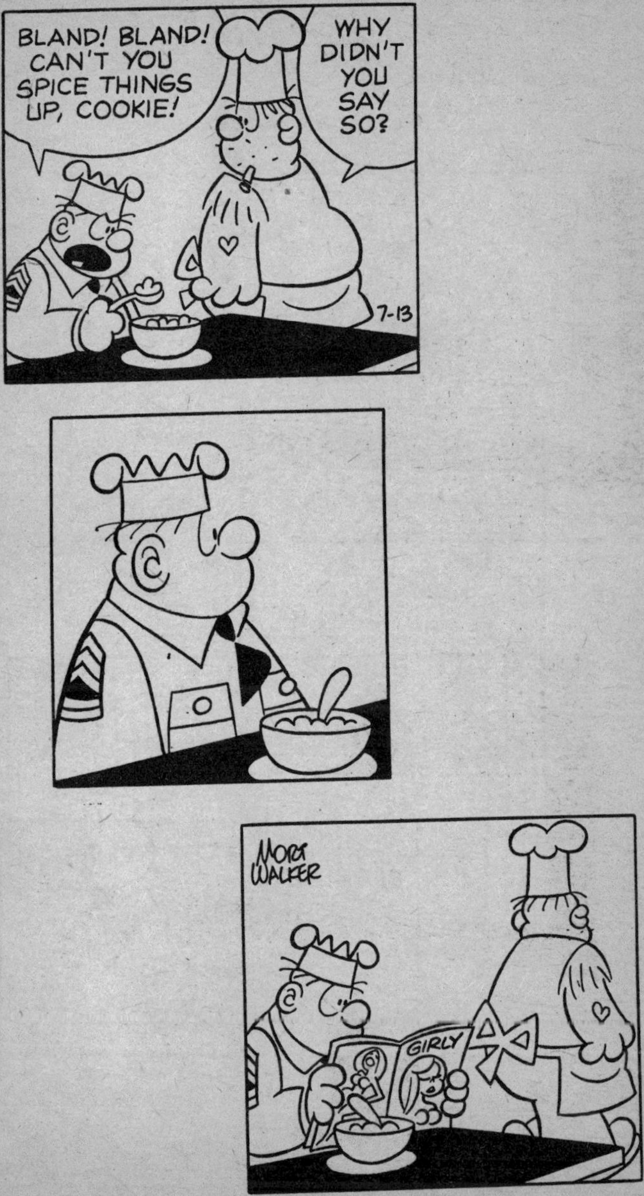
BLAND! BLAND! CAN'T YOU SPICE THINGS UP, COOKIE!
WHY DIDN'T YOU SAY SO?
7-13
MORT WALKER
GIRLY

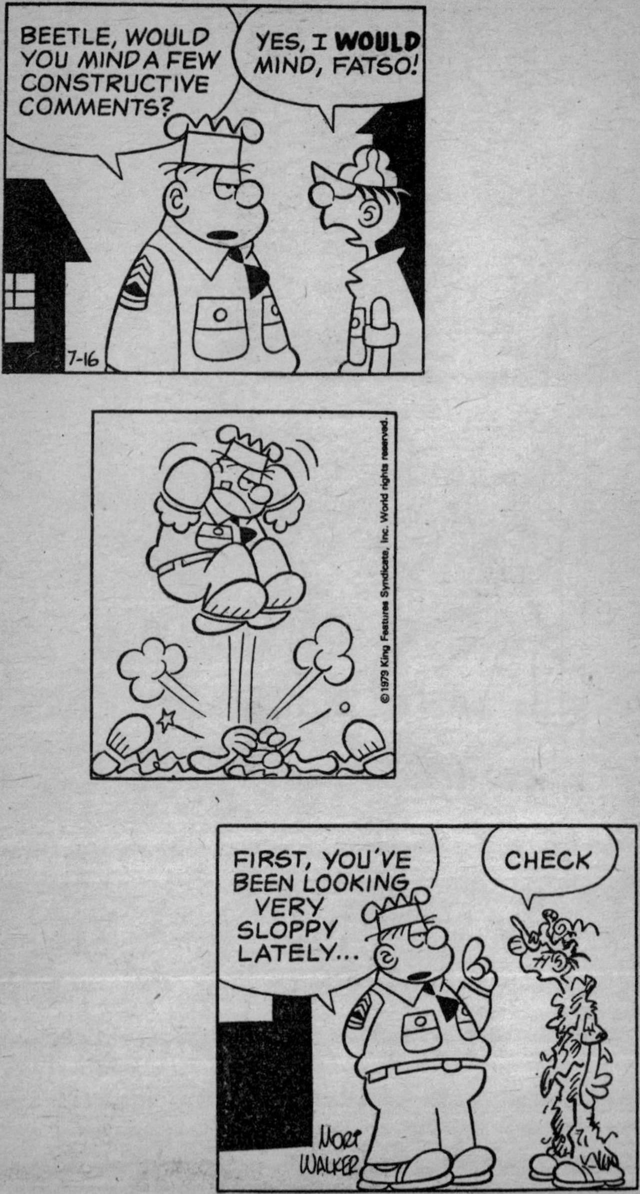
BEETLE, WOULD YOU MIND A FEW CONSTRUCTIVE COMMENTS?
YES, I **WOULD** MIND, FATSO!
7-16
FIRST, YOU'VE BEEN LOOKING VERY SLOPPY LATELY...
CHECK
MORT WALKER

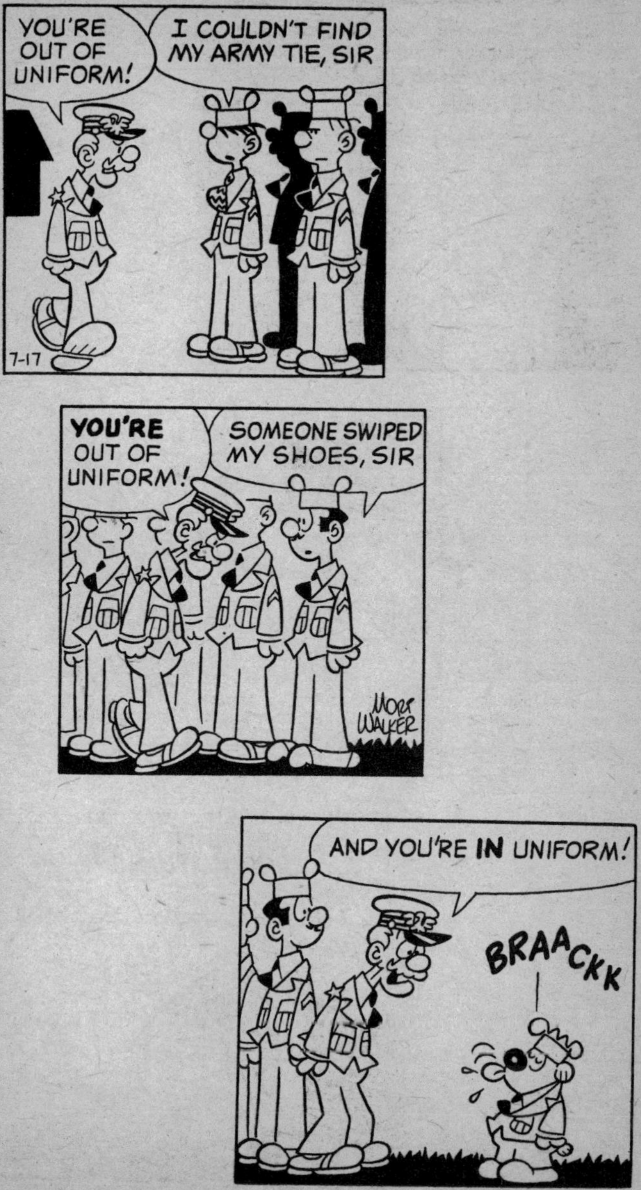
YOU'RE OUT OF UNIFORM!
I COULDN'T FIND MY ARMY TIE, SIR
7-17
YOU'RE OUT OF UNIFORM!
SOMEONE SWIPED MY SHOES, SIR
MORT WALKER
AND YOU'RE IN UNIFORM!
BRAACKK

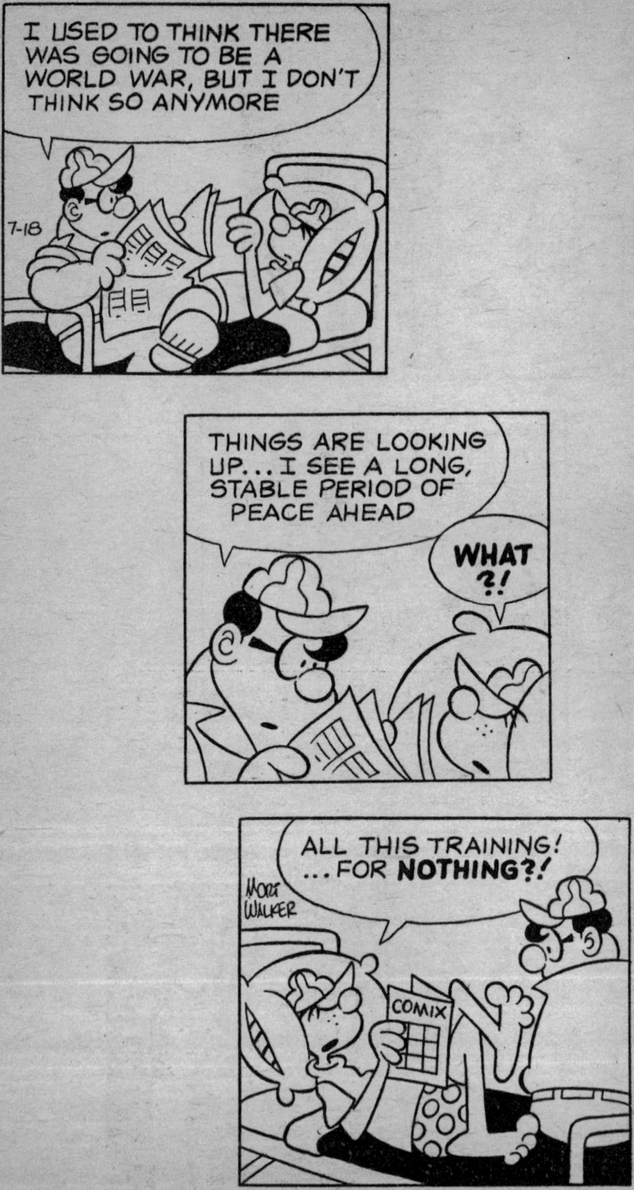

I USED TO THINK THERE WAS GOING TO BE A WORLD WAR, BUT I DON'T THINK SO ANYMORE
7-18
THINGS ARE LOOKING UP... I SEE A LONG, STABLE PERIOD OF PEACE AHEAD
WHAT ?!
ALL THIS TRAINING! ...FOR NOTHING?!
MORT WALKER
COMIX

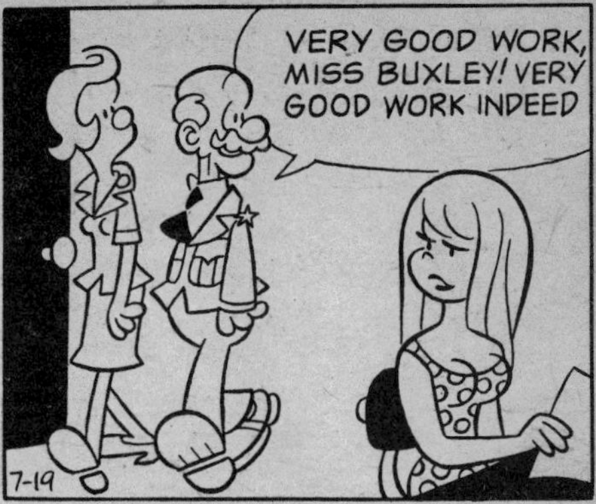
VERY GOOD WORK, MISS BUXLEY! VERY GOOD WORK INDEED
7-19

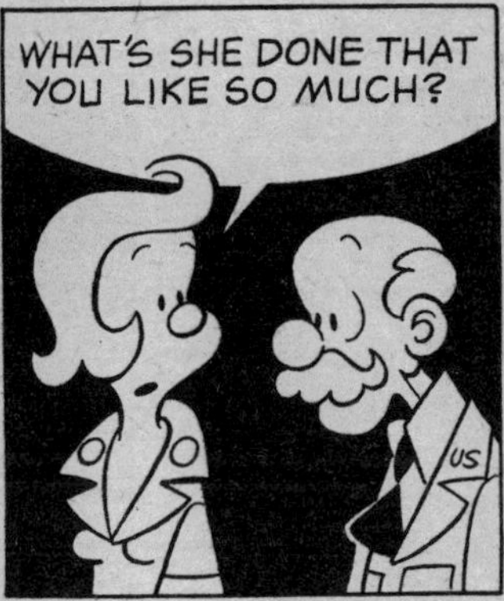
WHAT'S SHE DONE THAT YOU LIKE SO MUCH?
US

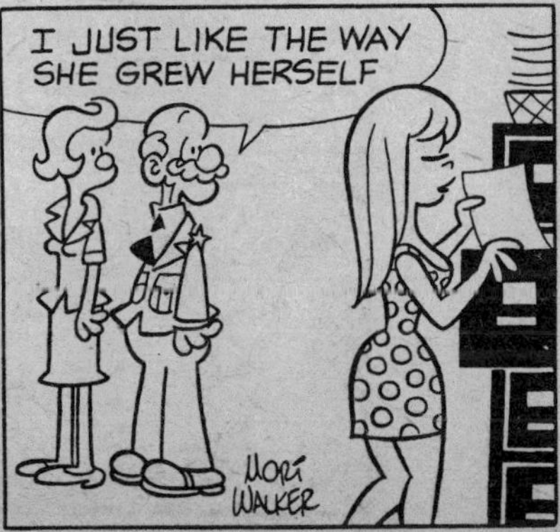
I JUST LIKE THE WAY SHE GREW HERSELF
MORT WALKER

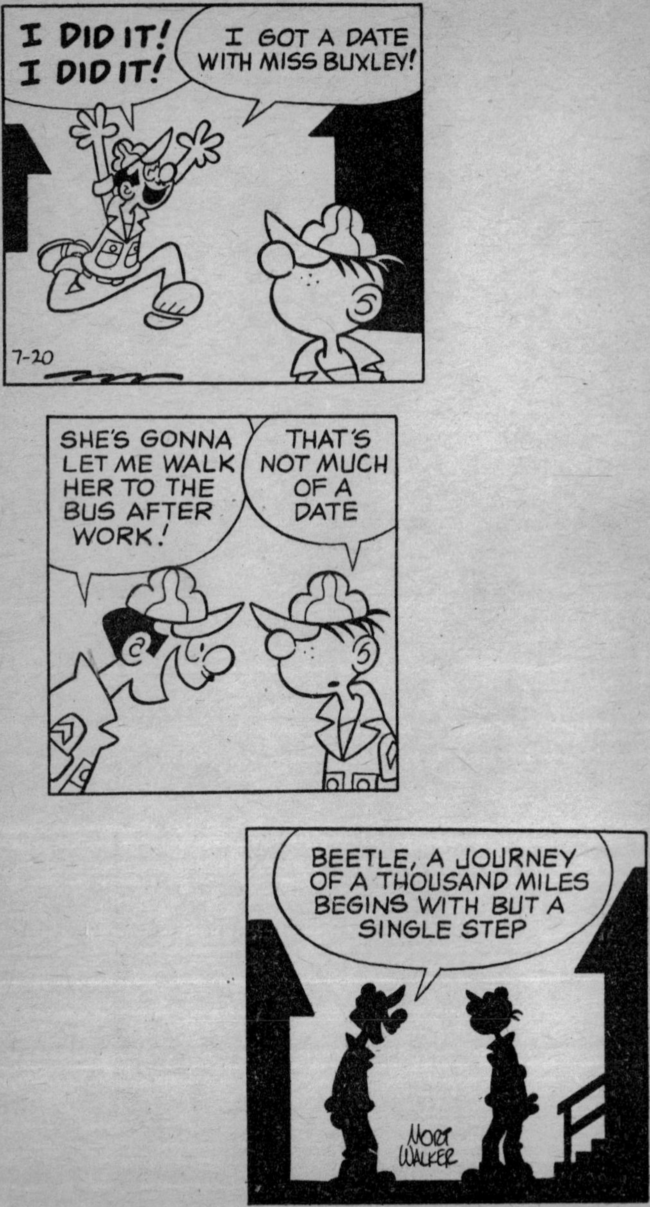
I DID IT! I DID IT!
I GOT A DATE WITH MISS BUXLEY!
7-20
SHE'S GONNA LET ME WALK HER TO THE BUS AFTER WORK!
THAT'S NOT MUCH OF A DATE
BEETLE, A JOURNEY OF A THOUSAND MILES BEGINS WITH BUT A SINGLE STEP
MORT WALKER